First Printing: 2018

ISBN: 978-0-9969033-2-5

G.P.L Publishing
http://www.lulu.com/spotlight/gplpublishing.com

Ordering Information:

Special discounts are available on quantity purchases by corporations, associations, educators, and others. For details, contact the publisher at the above listed address.

Table of Contents

Tests and Quizzes Edition

Unit 1: Car and Ramp Benchmark (First Quiz, First Quiz Re-take and Second Quiz)

Learning Targets:

Reason quantitatively and use units to solve problems - Ch. 4.1
Create equations that describe numbers or relationships – Ch. 5.3, Ch. 5.2, Ch. 5.5
Represent and solve equations graphically - Ch. 1.6,
Analyze functions using different representations – S.ID.8
Interpret expressions for functions in terms of the situation they model – S.ID.8,
Understand solving equations as a process of reasoning and explain the reasoning – S.ID.8
Summarize represent, and interpret data on two categorical and quantitative variables – Ch. 1.6, Ch. 4.2
Interpret linear models – S.ID.8

4.0 Mastery	Ch. 1.6 – Students can accurately solve complete a table filling in the correct domain, function, and range rounding to the exact decimal place with no errors. Ch. 5.1 – Students can formulate a Slope using Slope formula from tabulated data with no errors. Ch. 5.2/5.3 - Students can Write an Equation of a Line in Slope-Intercept Form with no errors. S.ID.8 - Students are able to explain the relevance of the correlation coefficient in context of the situation presented and make predictions accordingly with no errors. Ch. 4.2 – Students can evaluate the correctness of a Linear Equation graphed from tabulated data with no errors. Ch. 5.5 – Students can Write Equations of Parallel and Perpendicular Lines and compare the connections between their slopes and can also identify the intersection point between two perpendicular lines with no errors.
	3.5 Progressing toward Mastery: Student shows qualities from both 3.0 and 4.0 with only 1 error.
3.0 Proficient	Ch. 1.6 – Students can complete a table filling in the correct domain, function, and range but do not consistently round to the correct decimal place with no more than 2 errors. Ch. 5.1 – Students can formulate a Slope using Slope formula from tabulated data with no errors. Ch. 5.2/5.3 - Students can Write an Equation of a Line in Slope-Intercept Form with no more than 2 errors. S.ID.8 - Students can accurately find the slope (a), y – intercept (b), and the correlation coefficient (r) of two variable data. Additionally, can adjust the graph "window" correctly to view the entire graph with no more than 2 errors. Ch. 4.2 – Students can differentiate between a correct and incorrect Linear Graph with no more than 2 errors. Ch. 5.5 – Students can Write Equations of Parallel and Perpendicular Lines with no more than 2 errors.
	2.5 Progressing toward Proficiency: There is no 2.5 for this exam.
2.0 Basic	Ch. 1.6 – Students can plug in the correct domain for problems regarding functions, but are not able to solve for the range. Ch. 5.1 – Students can correctly set up the Slope Form using Slope Formula. Ch. 5.2/5.3 - Students can identify basic components needed to Write an Equation of a Line in Slope-Intercept form. S.ID.8 - Students can interpret the slope (a), y – intercept (b), and the correlation coefficient (r) of two variable data. Ch. 4.2 – Students can describe the process of graphing a Linear equation. Ch. 5.5 – Students are not able to correctly distinguish between Parallel and Perpendicular lines.
	1.5 Progressing towards Basic **Partial knowledge of the 2.0 content, but major errors or omissions regarding the 3.0 content.**
Score 1.0	**With HELP partial knowledge understanding of some of the SIMPLER details.**

Name_____ Period_____ Date_____

Unit 1: Car and Ramp (First Quiz)

This quiz covers the following chapters:
5.1 - Slope Formula
5.2/5.3 - Slope - Intercept Form
Statistics - Linear Regression
1.6 - Represent Functions as Rules and Tables
5.5 - Parallel/Perpendicular Lines

My name is _____, my signature states that all answers on this test are my own. My signature shows that I was honest in taking this quiz and in no way cheated to obtain any answer. Note: If you do not sign this document it shows me you did not want to be trustworthy, therefore, I will not grade it.

Ch. 5.1/5.2/5.3

Derive an equation from the table below, make sure your final answer is in slope - intercept form "y = mx + b".

Fat you eat (g)	31	39	19	34	43	39	35
Calories you gain	580	680	410	590	660	640	570

Show all work below.

Use the table from the previous page to complete L$_1$ and L$_2$

L$_1$	L$_2$

Linear Regression Using Technology (S.ID.8)

Calculator Window

Xmin =   Xscl =   Ymax =   Xres =

Xmax =   Ymin =   Yscl =

Linear Regression/Line of best fit
(Write Linear Regression Equation below (for y) subsituting values)
a =

b =

y =

r =

In the space to the below, elaborate on what the numerical value of the correlation coefficient means in context to your data.

_____

_____

Push the "Y=" button now plug the equation you derived on **Page 88** into your calculator for (Y$_2$). Once that is completed push the "graph" button to compare **your** equation versus the **calculator's** linear regression.
Find me when finished to be checked off.

My box to check off.

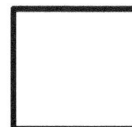

Chapter 1.6

Use the equation you derived from **Page 88** to complete the table below.

Domain: Start by 40, then count by 10's

Domain	Function	Range

Show all work for each one of your answers. If an answer does not need work to be shown make sure you explain in detail why your choice is correct. If I do not understand how you got the correct answer I will automatically mark it incorrect.

Circle the entire letter and answer of your choice.

I). Which equation represents the line that passes through (1, 1) and is perpendicular to the line passing through (2, 3) and (1, 5)?

II). What is the equation of the vertical line that passes through (6, - 2)

A). y = - 2

B). y = 6

C). x = 6

D). x = - 2

III). Which statement is true of the given lines?
Line a: 3x - 4y = - 4
Line b: 3x - 4y = 8
Line c: 3x + 4y = 8

A) Lines a and b are parallel
B) Lines a and c are parallel
C) Lines b and c are parallel
D) Lines a and c are perpendicular
E) Lines a and b are perpendicular

Grading Scales for all Chapters Covered in this Benchmark

- This is how I am grading this quiz. Do not worry about these pages until after I grade it.

- Refer to the scale passed out for this quiz to understand <u>exactly</u> what is passing for each chapter.

- Remember, there is <u>No</u> reason to guess in this classroom. The scale tells you what you need to do on each chapter to be a Level 4.

Chapter 5.1: Slope Formula - Page 88

4	3.5	3	2.5	2	1.5	1

Chapter 5.2/5.3: Slope Intercept Form - Page 88

4	3.5	3	2.5	2	1.5	1

Linear Regression Using Technology: S.ID.8 - Page 89

4	3.5	3	2.5	2	1.5	1

Chapter 1.6: Domain/Function/Range - Page 90

4	3.5	3	2.5	2	1.5	1

Chapter 5.5: Parallel/Perpendicular Lines - Page 91

4	3.5	3	2.5	2	1.5	1

Name_____Period_____ Date_____

Unit 1: Car and Ramp (First Quiz) - Retake

This quiz covers the following chapters:
5.1 - Slope Formula
5.2/5.3 - Slope - Intercept Form
Statistics - Linear Regression
1.6 - Represent Functions as Rules and Tables
5.5 - Parallel/Perpendicular Lines

My name is _____, my signature states that all answers on this test are my own. My signature shows that I was honest in taking this quiz and in no way cheated to obtain any answer. Note: If you do not sign this document it shows me you did not want to be trustworthy, therefore, I will not grade it.

Ch. 5.1/5.2/5.3

Derive an equation from the table below, make sure your final answer is in slope - intercept form "y = mx + b".

The number of facebook friends you have	53	19	24	17	95	68	23
The number of people that actually like you	50	27	187	84	143	216	45

Show all work below.

Use the table from the previous page to complete L_1 and L_2

Linear Regression Using Technology (S.ID.8)

L_1	L_2

Calculator Window

Xmin =   Xscl =   Ymax =   Xres =

Xmax =   Ymin =   Yscl =

Linear Regression/Line of best fit
(Write Linear Regression Equation below (for y) subsituting values)

a =

b =

y =

r =

In the space to the below, elaborate on what the numerical value of the correlation coefficient means in context to your data.

_____

_____

Push the "Y=" button now plug the equation you derived on **Page 93** into your calculator for (Y_2). Once that is completed push the "graph" button to compare **your** equation versus the **calculator's** linear regression.
Find me when finished to be checked off.

My box to check off.

Use the equation you derived from **Page 93** to complete the table below.

Domain: Start by 100, then count by 20's

Domain	Function	Range

- List the domain:

- List the range:

- Find y' when x = 220   Ordered Pair: **(,   )**

(Show all work below; state your ordered pair in context)

Circle the entire letter and answer of your choice.

I). - Illustrate all ways in which you
were able to answer this question.

What is the line that passes
through (-8, 0)

A). $y = -8$ B). $x = 0$ C). y - axis   D). x - axis

II). You will need the graph below to better answer this question. Let's say you are
walking on a straight line designated by the ordered pairs (- 2, - 2) and (- 4, 2). At
a certain point you change your mind and want to walk a line perpendicular to the
one above that goes through the point (1, 5)

1) Graph both equations on the graph provided (use a table like Ch. 1.6 if you
forgothow to graph in slope - intercept form). Extend all points until both graphs
intersect.

2) Show all work needed to find the original equation and the perpendicular
equation on the next page.
(Box both answers when complete)

3) Perpendicular equations cross to form _____.

4) What is the intersection point of both equations on your graph? (,   )

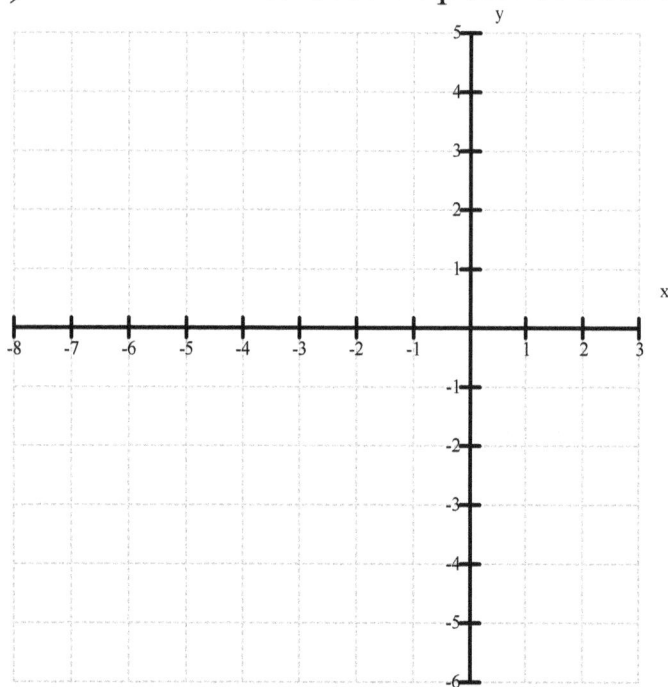

Additional space to complete problem II on page 96.

Grading Scales for all Chapters Covered in this Benchmark

- This is how I am grading this quiz. Do not worry about these pages until after I grade it.

- Refer to the scale passed out for this quiz to understand <u>exactly</u> what is passing for each chapter.

- Remember, there is <u>No</u> reason to guess in this classroom. The scale tells you what you need to do on each chapter to be a Level 4.

Chapter 5.1: Slope Formula - Page 93

4	3.5	3	2.5	2	1.5	1

Chapter 5.2/5.3: Slope - Intercept Form - Page 93

4	3.5	3	2.5	2	1.5	1

Linear Regression Using Technology: S.ID.8 - Page 94

4	3.5	3	2.5	2	1.5	1

Chapter 1.6: Domain/Function/Range - Page 95

4	3.5	3	2.5	2	1.5	1

Chapter 5.5: Parallel/Perpendicular Lines - Page 96

4	3.5	3	2.5	2	1.5	1

Blank Page for notes, thoughts,

Or drawings.

Name_____ Period_____ Date_____

Unit 1: Car and Ramp (Quiz 2)

This quiz covers the following chapters:
5.1 - Slope Formula
5./5.32 - Slope - Intercept form
Statistics - Linear Regression
1.6 - Represent Functions as Rules and Tables
5.5 - Parallel/Perpendicular lines

My name is _____, my signature states that all answers on this test are my own. My signature shows that I was honest in taking this quiz and in no way cheated to obtain any answer. Note: If you do not sign this document it shows me you did not want to be trustworthy, therefore, I will not grade it.

Ch. 5.1/5.2/5.3

Derive an equation from the table below, make sure your final answer is in slope - intercept form "y = mx + b".

Students enrolled	99	110	113	116	138	174	220
Teachers	1128	1290	1356	1478	1480	1521	2075

Show all work below.

Use the table from the previous page to complete L_1 and L_2

Linear Regression Using Technology (S.ID.8)

L_1	L_2

Calculator Window

Xmin =   Xscl =   Ymax =   Xres =

Xmax =   Ymin =   Yscl =

Linear Regression/Line of best fit
(Write Linear Regression Equation below (for y)
subsituting values)

a =

b =

y =

r =

In the space to the below, elaborate on what the numerical value of the correlation coefficient means in context to your data.

_____

_____

Push the "Y=" button now plug the equation you derived on **Page 100** into your calculator for (Y_2). Once that is completed push the "graph" button to compare **your** equation versus the **calculator's** linear regression.
Find me when finished to be checked off.

My box to check off.

Chapter 1.6

Use the equation you derived from **Page 100** to complete the table below.

Domain: Start by 280, then count by 15's

Domain	Function	Range

- List the domain:

- List the range:

- Find y' when x = 120   Ordered Pair: **(,   )**

(Show all work below; state your ordered pair in context)

Circle the entire letter and answer of your choice.

I). In the empty space to the right, provide a visual illustration to further prove your selection below.

What is the line that passes through (0 , - 4)

A). $x = - 4$ B). $x = 0$ C). The origin   D). x - axis

II). You will need the graph below to better answer this question. Let's say you are walking on a straight line designated by the ordered pairs (- 3, - 1) and (- 1, 0). At a certain point you change your mind and want to walk a line perpendicular to the ordered pairs above that goes through the point (- 6, 4)

1) Graph both equations on the graph provided (use a table like Ch. 1.6, slope intercept form, or plot points and just use the slope). Extend all points until both graphs intersect.

2) Show all work needed to find the original equation and the perpendicular equation. (Show all work on the next page.)

3) The product of your two perpendicular slopes is _____. (Show the work on the line provided)

4) What is the intersection point of both equations on your graph? (Use Pg. _____ instructions on the car and ramp to help you use the calculator for this answer.) (Check your solutions below or on a separate sheet of paper)

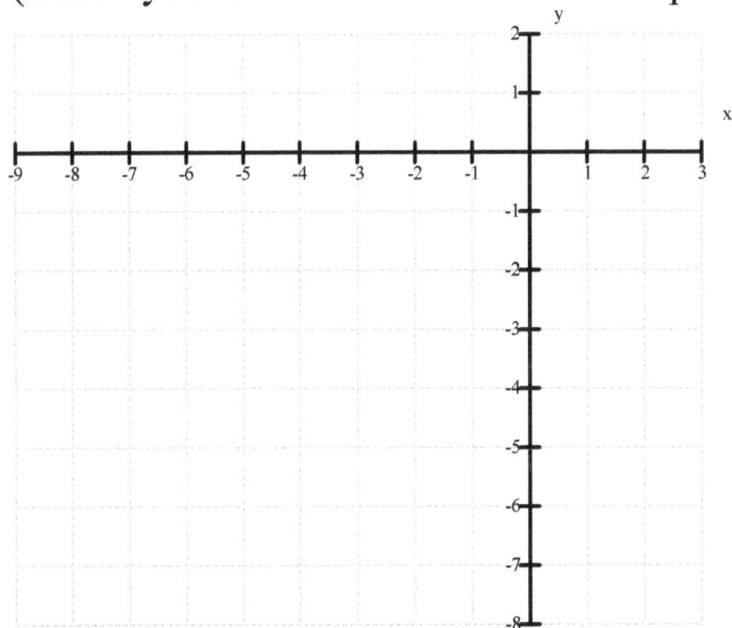

Additional space to complete problem II on page 103.

Grading Scales for all Chapters Covered in this Benchmark

- This is how I am grading this quiz. Do not worry about these pages until after I grade it.

- Refer to the scale passed out for this quiz to understand <u>exactly</u> what is passing for each chapter.

- Remember, there is <u>No</u> reason to guess in this classroom. The scale tells you what you need to do on each chapter to be a Level 4.

Chapter 5.1: Slope Formula - Page 100

4	3.5	3	2.5	2	1.5	1

Chapter 5.2/5.3: Slope - Intercept Form - Page 100

4	3.5	3	2.5	2	1.5	1

Linear Regression Using Technology: S.ID.8 - Page 101

4	3.5	3	2.5	2	1.5	1

Chapter 1.6: Domain/Function/Range - Page 102

4	3.5	3	2.5	2	1.5	1

Chapter 5.5: Parallel/Perpendicular Lines - Page 103

4	3.5	3	2.5	2	1.5	1

	Unit 1: Car and Ramp Benchmark – Ch. 5.5 and Ch. 7.2 Quiz

Learning Targets:

Create equations that describe numbers or relationships – Ch. 5.5
Represent and solve equations and inequalities graphically – Ch. 5.5, Ch. 7.2
Understand solving equations as a process of reasoning and explain the reasoning - Ch. 7.2
Solve systems of equations – Ch. 7.2
Interpret linear models – Ch. 5.5, Ch. 7.2

4.0 Mastery	-Ch. 5.5 (Deriving Perpendicular Equation): Students can derive the correct perpendicular equation given an original equation and a point. -Ch. 5.5 (Graphs of Original and Perpendicular Equations): Students are able to graph the original and perpendicular equations correctly. The original and perpendicular graphs have at least 4 points on each with correctly labeled ordered pairs. -Ch. 7.2 (Solving Linear Systems - Algebraically): Students are able to find the correct intersection point of the original and perpendicular equations algebraically. Intersection point matches both graphical and calculator work. -Ch. 7.2 (Solving Linear Systems - Graphically): Students are able to find the correct intersection point of the original and perpendicular equations graphically. Intersection point matches both algebraic and calculator work. -Ch. 7.2 (Solving Linear Systems – Graphing Calculator Work): Students are able to find the correct intersection point of the original and perpendicular equations using the Graphing Calculator. Intersection point matches both algebraic and graphical work.
	3.5 Progressing toward Mastery: Student only makes 1 mistake in any of the above content areas
3.0 Proficient	-Ch. 5.5 (Deriving Perpendicular Equation): Students can derive the correct perpendicular equation given an original equation and a point with at most 2 errors. -Ch. 5.5 (Graphs of Original and Perpendicular Equations): Students are able to graph the original and perpendicular equations correctly. The original and perpendicular graphs have at least 2 points on each with correctly labeled ordered pairs. -Ch. 7.2 (Solving Linear Systems by Substitution Method – Algebraically): Students are able to correctly find the intersection point of the original and perpendicular equation algebraically with at most 2 errors. Intersection point matches both graphical and calculator work. -Ch. 7.2 (Solving Linear Systems - Graphically): Students are able to find the correct intersection point of the original and perpendicular equations graphically with at most 2 errors. Intersection point matches both algebraic and calculator work. -Ch. 7.2 (Solving Linear Systems – Graphing Calculator Work): Students are able to find the correct intersection point of the original and perpendicular equations using the Graphing Calculator with at most 2 errors. Intersection point matches both algebraic and graphical work.
	2.5 Progressing toward Proficiency: No 2.5 for this exam.

2.0 Basic	-Ch. 5.5 (Deriving Perpendicular Equation): Students was not able to derive the correct perpendicular equation given an original equation and a point due to more than 2 errors. -Ch. 5.5 (Graphs of Original and Perpendicular Equations): Students were not able to graph the original and perpendicular equations correctly. The original and perpendicular graphs only have 1 point on each with correctly labeled ordered pairs. -Ch. 7.2 (Solving Linear Systems by Substitution Method – Algebraically): Students are not able to correctly find the intersection point of the original and perpendicular equation algebraically. Student has more than 2 errors in attempting to find the solution. -Ch. 7.2 (Solving Linear Systems - Graphically): Students are not able to find the correct intersection point of the original and perpendicular equations graphically. Student has more than 2 errors in attempting to find the solution. -Ch. 7.2 (Solving Linear Systems – Graphing Calculator Work): Students are not able to find the correct intersection point of the original and perpendicular equations using the Graphing Calculator. Student has more than 2 errors in attempting to find the solution.
	1.5 Progressing towards Basic **Partial knowledge of the 2.0 content, but major errors or omissions regarding the 3.0 content.**
Score 1.0	**With HELP partial knowledge understanding of some of the SIMPLER details.**

Pg. 118

Name_____Date_____ Period_____

My name is _____, my signature states that all answers on this test are my own. My signature shows that I was honest in taking this quiz and in no way cheated to obtain any answer. Note: If you do not sign this document it shows me you did not want to be trustworthy, therefore, I will not grade it.

This is a 1 problem exam. You will have 40 minutes for this exam.
The instructions for each individual part as as follows:

Chapter 5.5
- Create a line perpendicular to the original equation provided

- Graph the original and perpendicular equations on the graph paper provided
(**plot and label at least 4 ordered pairs on each line** - no matter what method you used to graph the lines)

Chapter 7.2
- Find the intersection point of both the original and perpendicular equation
(**show all work by hand**)

- Label the intersection point of both equations **on the graph paper** provided
(make sure your 4 ordered pairs for each equation are labeled)

- Show the intersection point using the **graphing calculator**
(make sure the screen on your calculator says "Intersection")

Deriving Parallel/Perpendicular Lines (Ch. 5.5)

Write an equation of a line that passed through point (0, 2), and is perpendicular to the equation $4x + 2y = 3$. Box your answer.

---

*Solving Systems of Equations Ch 7.2 **(Finding intersection points)***
(Show all of your work on this page and the next page)

Solution:

Using Technology to Aid With Solving Systems of Equations

Equation of Original Line

Equation of Perpendicular Line

_____

_____

L_1	L_2

This box is here to help you
with graphing the equation.

Calculator Window

Xmin =

Xmax =

Xscl =

Ymin =

Ymax =

Yscl =

Xres =

L_1	L_3

This box is here to help you
with graphing the equation.

Once you have plugged in all the data above into your calculator select "GRAPH". You should see both sets of points with lines going through them. If you do not see them, be creative and find a way, if that does not work then ask me. Once you see both, select "2nd", then "TRACE". This will send you to "CALC" which sets up different components to solve for. Select "5" - Intersection (which is the solution to both graphs). Move your cursor near the intersection using the arrow keys and hit enter 3 times.

Write the solution rounded to the hundredths place below.

Solution:

How close is your solution to the calculator's? Calculate the differences in x - values and y - values and write the findings below. **Find me when finished to be checked off.**

Differences in x-values:

My box to check off.

Differences in y-values:

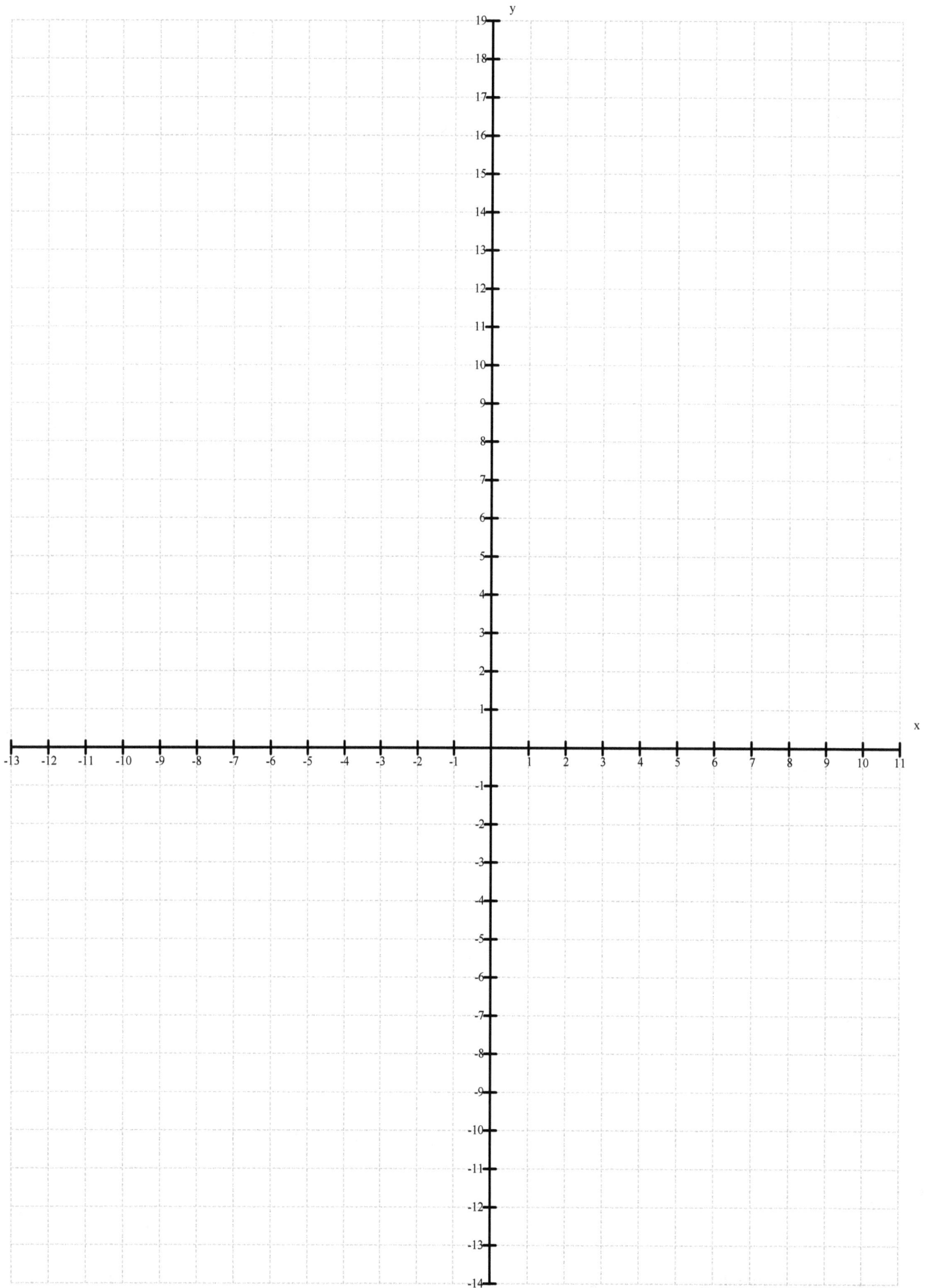

Grading Scales for all Chapters Covered in this Benchmark

- This is how I am grading this quiz. Do not worry about these pages until after I grade it.

- Refer to the scale passed out for this quiz to understand <u>exactly</u> what is passing for each chapter.

- Remember, there is <u>No</u> reason to guess in this classroom. The scale tells you what you need to do on each chapter to be a Level 4.

Chapter 5.5: Deriving Perpendicular Equation - Page 119

4	3.5	3	2.5	2	1.5	1

Chapter 5.5: Graphs of Original and Perpendicular Equations - Page 122

4	3.5	3	2.5	2	1.5	1

Chapter 7.2: Solving Linear Systems (Algebraically) - Pages 119 & 120

4	3.5	3	2.5	2	1.5	1

Chapter 7.2: Solving Linear Systems (Graphically) - Page 122

4	3.5	3	2.5	2	1.5	1

Chapter 7.2: Solving Linear Systems (Graphing Calculator Work) - Page 121

4	3.5	3	2.5	2	1.5	1

Unit 1: Car and Ramp Benchmark (Third Quiz)

Learning Targets:

Create equations that describe numbers or relationships – Ch. 5.5
Represent and solve equations and inequalities graphically
Understand the concept of a function and use function notation – Ch. 4.7
Interpret expressions for functions in terms of the situation they model
Understand solving equations as a process of reasoning and explain the reasoning
Solve systems of equations – Ch. 7.2
Interpret linear models

4.0 Mastery	Ch. 5.5 – Students can correctly Write Equations of Perpendicular Lines provided ordered pairs. Also, student can correctly graph two perpendicular lines and identify their intersection point. Additionally, student can identify and illustrate vertical or horizontal lines that pass through a specified point. Ch. 7.2 – Students can correctly solve Linear Systems algebraically and state the solution in context. Ch. 7.2 – Student can correctly solve Linear Systems by using technology. Ch. 4.7 – Students can correctly evaluate for (x) and solve for (x) in function notation. Also, student can correctly state the symbols as questions and explain their answers in context.
	3.5 Progressing toward Mastery: Student shows qualities from both 3.0 and 4.0.
3.0 Proficient	Ch. 5.5 – Students can Write Equations of Perpendicular Lines provided ordered pairs. Also, student can correctly graph two perpendicular lines. Additionally, student can identify vertical or horizontal lines that pass through a specified point. Ch. 7.2 – Students can correctly solve Linear Systems algebraically but do not state the solution in context. Ch. 7.2 – Student can input the proper data into the calculator but need a little help with finding the "intersection point" using technology. Ch. 4.7 – Students can correctly evaluate for (x), but makes small errors in solving for (x) in function notation. Student makes slight errors when stating the symbols as questions and explaining their answers in context.
	2.5 Progressing toward Proficiency: Student shows qualities from both 2.0 and 3.0.
2.0 Basic	Ch. 5.5 – Student has difficulty writing Equations of Perpendicular Lines provided ordered pairs. Also students are not able to properly graph the perpendicular lines (due to equations not being properly written). Lastly, students do not accurately graph a vertical or horizontal line through a specified point. Ch. 7.2 – Students are able to set up the linear system properly, but, they are only able to solve for one variable or solve both variables incorrectly. Ch. 7.2 – Students have difficulty inputting the proper data into the calculator; therefore, they are not able to find the "intersection point". They are able to show both graphs using technology. Ch. 4.7 – Students have difficulty evaluating for (x), and solving for (x) in function notation. Student is not able to state the symbols as questions and explain their answers in context.
	1.5 Progressing towards Basic **Partial knowledge of the 2.0 content, but major errors or omissions regarding the 3.0 content.**
Score 1.0	**With HELP partial knowledge understanding of some of the SIMPLER details.**

Name_____Period_____ Date_____

Unit 1: Car and Ramp (Third Quiz)

This quiz covers the following chapters:

5.5 - Parallel/Perpendicular lines
7.2 - Solving Systems of Equations by Substitution
4.7 - Function Notation

My name is _____, my signature states that all answers on this test are my own. My signature shows that I was honest in taking this quiz and in no way cheated to obtain any answer. Note: If you do not sign this document it shows me you did not want to be trustworthy, therefore, I will not grade it.

Ch 5.5

I). You will need the graph below to better answer this question. Let's say you are driving on a straight line designated by the ordered pairs (2, 0) and (4, 4). At a certain point you change your mind and want to drive a line perpendicular to the one above that goes through the point (- 2, 3). **x is the number of minutes, y is the distance driven in miles**.

1) Graph both equations on the graph provided (use a table like Ch. 1.6 if you forgot how to graph in slope - intercept form). Extend all points until both graphs intersect.

2) Show all work needed to find the **Original Equation** (#1), and the **Perpendicular Equation** (#2). Box both answers when complete.

3) Write the intersection point of both equations from your graph?_____

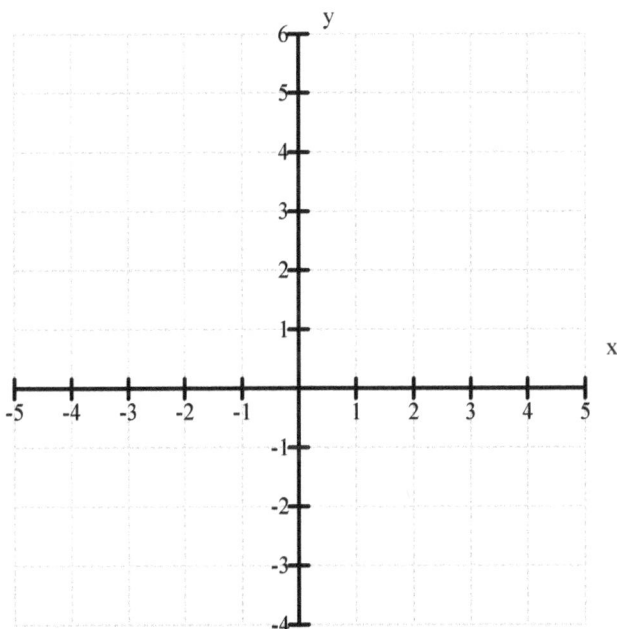

Chapter 5.5

Circle the entire letter and answer of your choice.

II). - Illustrate all ways in which you
were able to answer this question.

What is the **line** that passes
through (1, 0)

A). y = 1   B). x = 1

C). x = 0   D). Y - axis

Chapter 7.2

You will use equations #1 and #2 from **Page 1** to prove the intersection point
on **Page 1**.

Original Equation #1_____

Perpendicular Equation #2_____

- Prove the intersection point of the two equations below.
- Box your ordered pair.
- State what your ordered pair means in context.

Solution in context:_____

Ch. 7.2 Using Technology to Aid With Solving Systems of Equations

Write the two equations from page 2 below, then type them into the "y =" button on your calculator.

Original Equation #1 _____ (Y_1)

Perpendicular Equation #2_____ (Y_2)

<u>Calculator Window</u>

Xmin =   Xmax =   Xscl =

Ymin =   Ymax =   Yscl =

Xres =

Once you have plugged in all the data above into your calculator select "GRAPH". You should see both sets of points with lines going through them. If you do not see them, be creative and find a way, if that does not work then ask me. Once you see both, select "2nd", then "TRACE". This will send you to "CALC" which sets up different components to solve for. Select "5" - Intersection (which is the solution to both graphs). Move your cursor near the intersection using the arrow keys and hit enter 3 times.

Write the solution rounded to the hundredths place below.

Solution:

How close is your solution to the calculator's? Calculate the differences in x - values and y - values and write the findings below. **Find me when finished to be checked off.**

Differences in x-values:

Differences in y-values:

My box to check off.

Chapter 4.7

Original Equation:_____

$D(x) = 128$ miles; $x =$

I) What does the above question say in words:_____

_____

II) Show all work needed to solve the problem below

Ordered Pair (,   )

Explain your answer in context:_____

_____

Perpendicular Equation: _____

$D(2) =$

I) What does the above question say in words:_____

_____

II) Show all work needed to solve the problem below

Ordered Pair (,   )

Explain your answer in context:_____

_____

Grading Scales for all Chapters Covered in this Benchmark

- This is how I am grading this quiz. Do not worry about these pages until after I grade it.

- Refer to the scale passed out for this quiz to understand <u>exactly</u> what is passing for each chapter.

- Remember, there is <u>No</u> reason to guess in this classroom. The scale tells you what you need to do on each chapter to be a Level 4.

Chapter 5.5: Parallel/Perpendicular Lines - Pages 139 and 140

4	3.5	3	2.5	2	1.5	1

Chapter 7.2: Solving Linear Systems by Substitution - Page 140

4	3.5	3	2.5	2	1.5	1

Chapter 7.2: Solving Linear Systems Using Technology - Page 141

4	3.5	3	2.5	2	1.5	1

Chapter 4.7: Function Notation - Page 142

4	3.5	3	2.5	2	1.5	1

Pg. 144

Blank Page for notes, thoughts,

Or drawings.

Unit 1: Car and Ramp Benchmark

Learning Targets:

Reason quantitatively and use units to solve problems - Ch. 4.1
Create equations that describe numbers or relationships – Ch. 5.1, Ch. 5.2, Ch. 5.3, Ch. 5.5
Represent and solve equations and inequalities graphically - Ch. 1.6, Ch. 4.2, Ch. 4.5
Understand the concept of a function and use function notation – Ch. 4.7
Analyze functions using different representations – Ch. 4.3, S.ID.8
Interpret expressions for functions in terms of the situation they model – S.ID.8, Ch. 4.5
Understand solving equations as a process of reasoning and explain the reasoning – Ch. 4.3, S.ID.8
Solve systems of equations – Ch. 7.2
Summarize represent, and interpret data on two categorical and quantitative variables – Ch. 1.6, Ch. 4.2, Ch. 4.5
Interpret linear models – S.ID.8, Ch. 4.5

4.0 Mastery	Ch. 1.6 – Students can solve and provide a written and/or verbal explanation using correct nomenclature regarding Functions and Tables. Ch. 4.1 – Students can choose the correct units and approximation of X/Y coordinates on a Cartesian Coordinate Plane. Ch. 5.1 – Students derive the slope using data from a table. Ch. 5.2/5.3 - Students can Write an Equation of a Line in Slope-Intercept Form S.ID.8 - Students are able to explain the relevance of the correlation coefficient in context of the situation presented and make predictions accordingly. Ch. 4.2 – Students can evaluate the correctness of a Linear Equation graphed from tabulated data. Ch. 5.5 – Students can Write Equations of Parallel and Perpendicular Lines and compare the connections between their slopes. Ch. 7.2 – Students can correctly solve Linear Systems algebraically and are able to access the "intersection function" using technology. Ch. 4.7 – Students can evaluate when and correctly solve for a function algebraically and with technology using function notation Ch. 4.7 - Students can evaluate when and correctly find the inverse of the function (solve for x) algebraically and with technology using function notation. Ch. 4.3 – Students can explain the relevance of intercepts in context of the situation. Ch. 4.4 – Students can accurately solve and provide a written and/or verbal explanation using correct nomenclature regarding Linear Graphs using Slope and Rate of Change. Ch. 4.5 – Students can correctly graph Linear Graphs using Slope-Intercept Form and visually show the "rise over run". Ch. 4.7 – Students can evaluate for position of photogate or speed given a linear graph and can use the correct vocabulary when providing an answer in context.
	3.5 Progressing toward Mastery: Student shows qualities from both 3.0 and 4.0.
3.0 Proficient	Ch. 1.6 – Students can accurately solve and create problems containing Functions and Tables. Ch. 4.1 – Students can choose the correct units and have very close approximations of X/Y coordinates on a Cartesian Coordinate Plane. Ch. 5.1 – Students can accurately find a slope using table from a data. Ch. 5.2/5.3 - Students can Write an Equation of a Line in Slope-Intercept Form given two points. S.ID.8 - Students can accurately find the slope (a), y – intercept (b), and the correlation coefficient (r) of two variable data. Additionally, can adjust the graph "window" correctly to view the entire graph. Ch. 4.2 – Students can differentiate between a correct and incorrect Linear Graph. Ch. 5.5 – Students can Write Equations of Parallel and Perpendicular Lines and deduct the connections between their slopes. Ch. 7.2 – Students can solve Linear Systems algebraically but need a little help with accessing the "intersection function" using technology. Ch. 4.7 – Students can evaluate when and correctly solve for a function either algebraically or with technology using function notation

		Ch. 4.7 - Students can evaluate when and correctly find the inverse of the function (solve for x) either algebraically or with technology using function notation. Ch. 4.3 – Students can accurately solve and/or graph linear equations by using X/Y intercepts. Ch. 4.4 – Students can accurately solve problems using Rate of Change. Also, the students can correctly graph linear equations by using rise over run (slope). Ch. 4.5 – Students can correctly graph Linear Graphs using Slope-Intercept Form. Ch. 4.7 – Students can evaluate for position of photogate or speed given a linear graph, but does not use all of the correct vocabulary when explaining its meaning in context.
		2.5 Progressing toward Proficiency: Student shows qualities from both 2.0 and 3.0.
2.0 Basic		Ch. 1.6 – Students can recognize problems containing Functions and Tables. Ch. 4.1 – Students can describe the correct units and approximation of X/Y coordinates on a Cartesian Coordinate Plane. Ch. 5.3 – Students can correctly set up the slope using data from a table. Ch. 5.2/5.3 - Students can identify basic components needed to Write an Equation of a Line in Slope-Intercept form. S.ID.8 - Students can interpret the slope (a), y – intercept (b), and the correlation coefficient (r) of two variable data. Ch. 4.2 – Students can describe the process of graphing a Linear equation. Ch. 5.5 – Students can explain the differences between Parallel and Perpendicular Lines. Ch. 7.2 – Students are able to set up the system properly. They are able to solve for one variable. They are able to show both graphs using technology. Ch. 4.7 – Students confuse evaluating for X with solving for X. Their attempt at technology was minimal. Ch. 4.7 - Students confuse solving for X with evaluating for X. Their attempt at technology was minimal. Ch. 4.3 – Students are able to compute X/Y intercepts. Ch. 4.4 – Students can determine the rise versus the run. Ch. 4.5 – Students can correctly interpret the rise and the run of a Linear Equation in Slope Intercept Form. Ch. 4.7 – Students does not correctly evaluate for position of photogate or speed given a linear graph and does not use the correct vocabulary when explaining its meaning in context.
		1.5 Progressing towards Basic **Partial knowledge of the 2.0 content, but major errors or omissions regarding the 3.0 content.**
Score 1.0		**With HELP partial knowledge understanding of some of the SIMPLER details.**

Blank Page for notes, thoughts,

Or drawings.

Car and Ramp Benchmark Individual Assessment Scenario 1

Position of Ramp	Position of Photogate (X-Coordinate)	Distance Traveled	2 Time Trials	Average Time Photogate	Speed of the car in "cm/s" (Y-Coordinate)
Hole 19	40				
Hole 19	50				
Hole 19	60				
Hole 19	70				

(Ch 1.6)

Label both your X and Y axes (same as the example)

Y - axis (count by 20's)

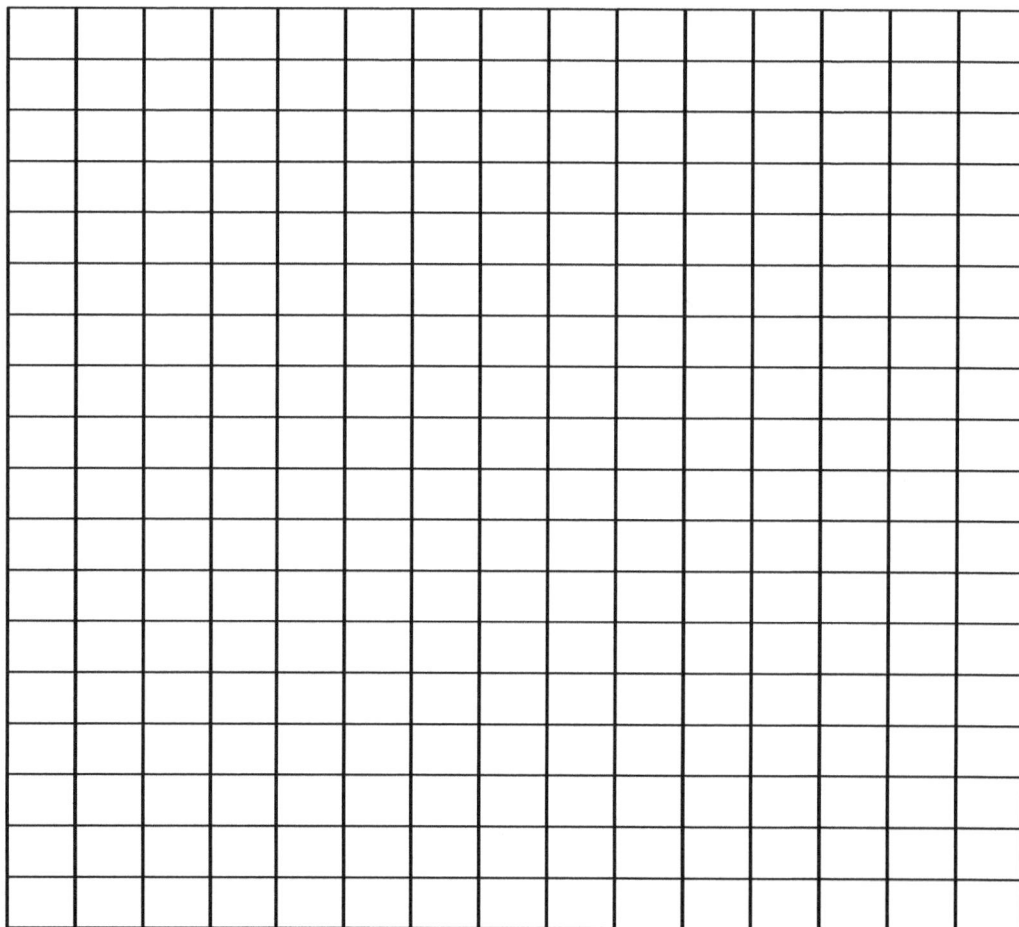

Y - axis

(Ch 4.1)

Label your ordered pairs on the graph

X - axis _____

X - axis (Count by 5's)

(Chapter 5.1) Using the table on the previous page, <u>**derive the slope**</u>. <u>**Show all work below and place your answer in the box**</u>.

> **Slope (m) =**

(Chapter 5.2/5.3) Using the slope above, formulate an equation in <u>**Slope-Intercept form.**</u> Show all work below and place your answer in the box.

> **Slope-Intercept form Answer using function notation (Ch 4.7):**

Line of Best Fit (Linear Regression) Using Technology (S.ID.8)

L_1	L_2

Calculator Window

Xmin =   Xscl =   Ymax =   Xres =

Xmax =   Ymin =   Yscl =

Line of Best Fit/Linear Regression
(Write Linear Regression Equation below (for y)
subsituting values)

a =

b =

y =

r =

In the space to the below, elaborate on the **relationship** between the numerical value of the correlation coefficient and what it means in context to your data.

_____

_____

_____

Push the "Y=" button now plug the equation you derived from the slope-intercept form on the bottom of Pg. 175 into the calculator for (Y_2). Once that is completed push the "graph" button to compare **your** equation versus the **calculator's** linear regression. **Find me when finished to be checked off.**

My box to check off.

Directions - Generate an equation based on the data below.
Photogate at 40 cm and Speed at 204 cm/s. Photogate at 50 cm and Speed at 228 cm/s.
- **Show mathematical work below.**

Original Equation using function notation Ch 5.5:

(Domain - Start from 0 and Count by 15's)
(Range - Round to the ones place)

Use the equation above
to complete the table below.

Domain	Function	Range

Graph the equation from Pg. 177 on the coordinate plane below.

Label your ordered pairs on the graph.

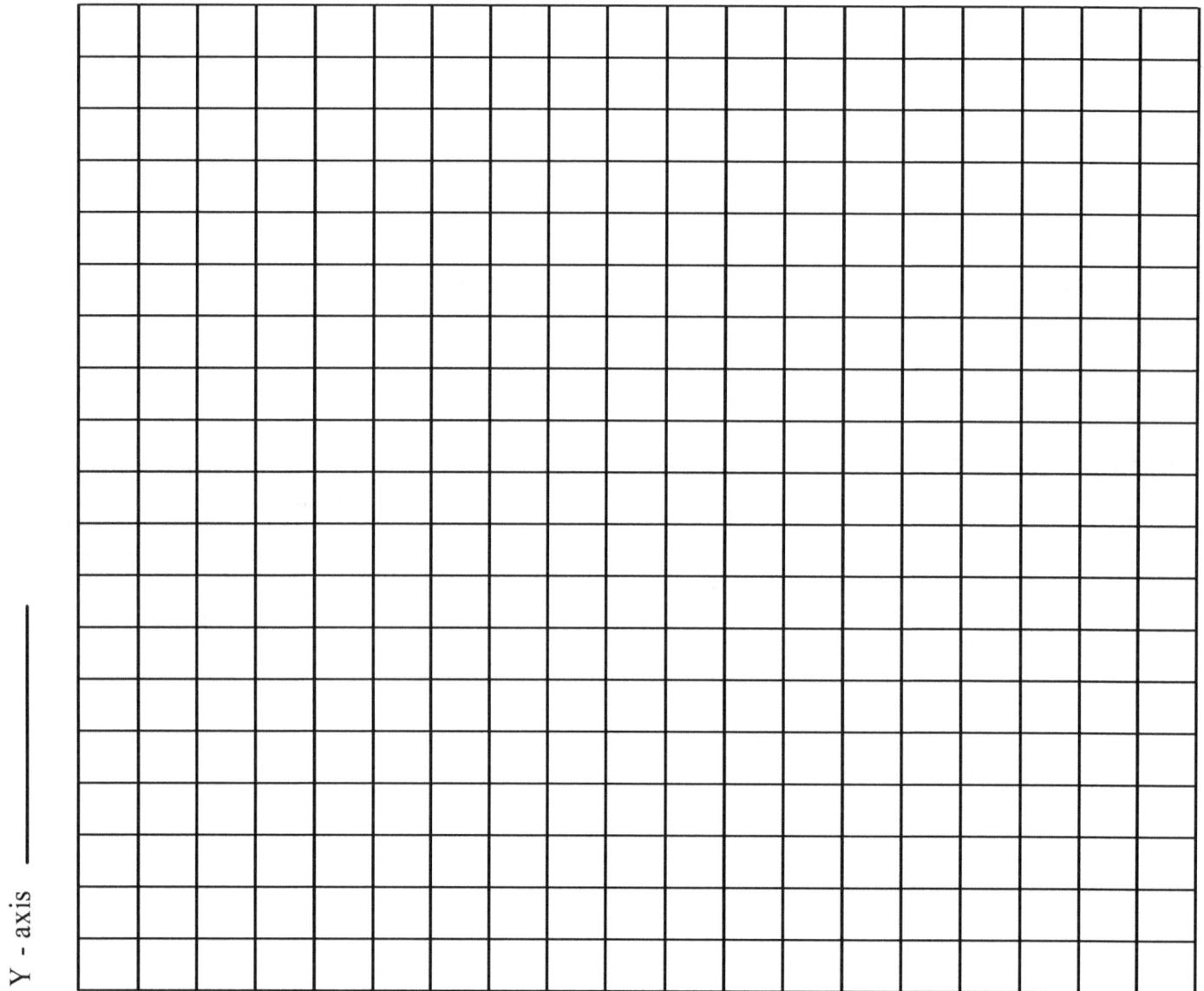

Y - axis

X - axis _____

(Hint - X-axis count by 5's
       Y-axis count by 10's)

Directions - Generate an equation **Parallel** to the one given to you on Pg. 177
that goes through a point with Photogate at 30 cm and Speed at 120 cm/s. **(Ch 5.5)**
- **Show mathematical work below.**

Parallel Line Equation using function notation Ch 5.5:

(Write in words below how you <u>know</u> your line is <u>parallel.</u>

(Domain - Start from 0 and Count by 15's)   *<u>Use the parallel equation</u>*
(Range - Round to the ones place)   *<u>above to complete the table below.</u>*

Domain	Function	Range

Pg. 180

First, graph the equation from Pg. 177 **again** on the coordinate plane below. Then, **Graph** the **parallel line equation** on the same coordinate plane using the **3 column table on the previous page.**

Label your ordered pairs on the graph. Ch 5.5

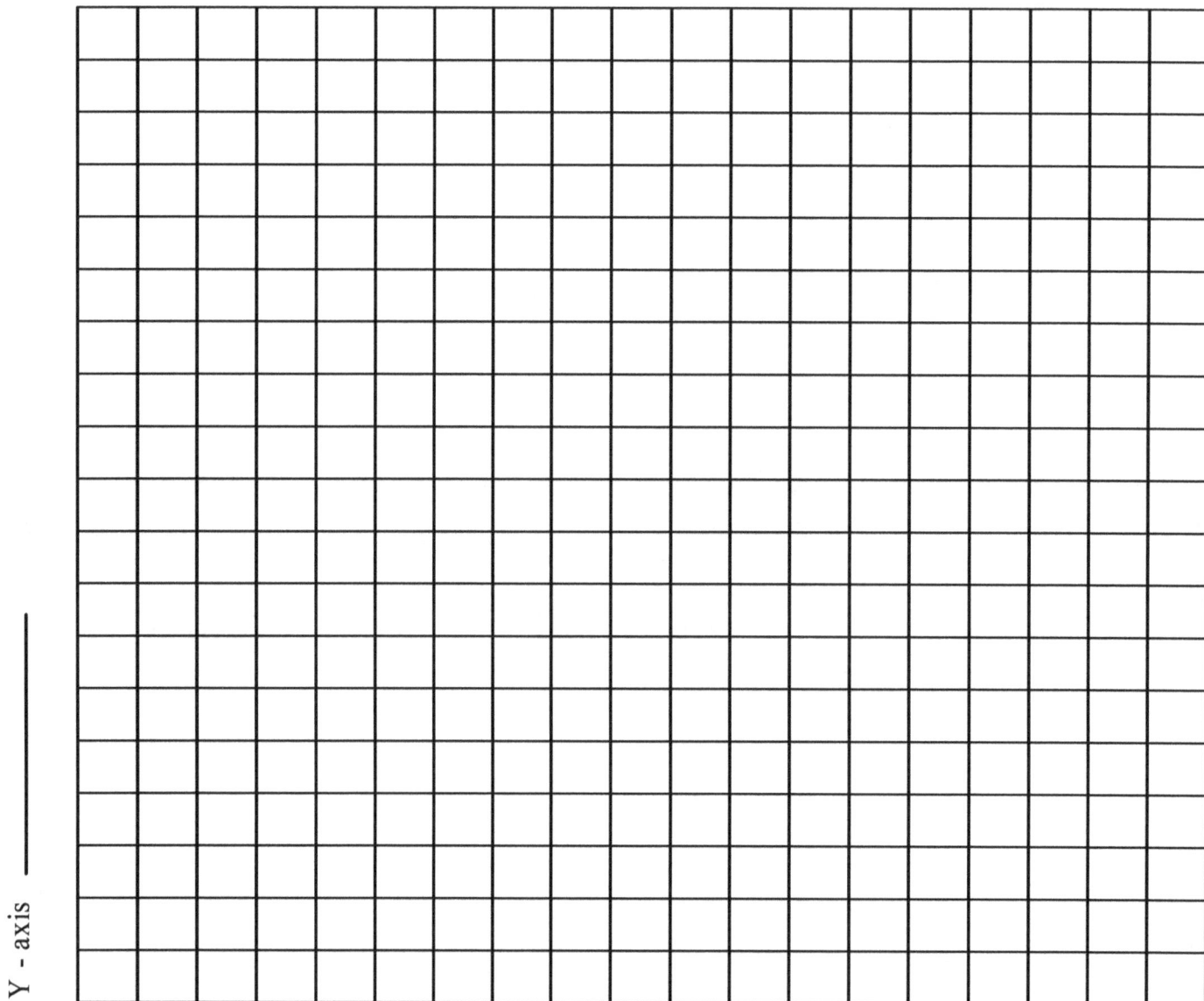

Y - axis

X - axis _____

(Hint - X-axis count by 5's
       Y-axis count by 10's)

Directions - Generate an equation **Perpendicular** to the one given to you on Pg. 177 that goes through a point with photogate at 70 cm and speed at 80 cm/s. **(Ch 5.5)**
- **Show mathematical work below.**

Perpendicular Line Equation using function notation Ch 5.5:

(**Write in words below how you <u>know</u> your line is <u>perpendicular</u>** - Also, what is the **product** of their slopes).

(Domain - Start from 0 and Count by 15's)
(Range - Round to the ones place)

<u>Use the perpendicular equation above to complete the table below.</u>

Domain	Function	Range

Pg. 182

First, graph the equation from Pg. 177 **again** on the coordinate plane below. Then, **Graph** the **perpendicular line equation** on the same coordinate plane using the **3 column table on the previous page.**

Label your ordered pairs on the graph (estimate the intersection point)

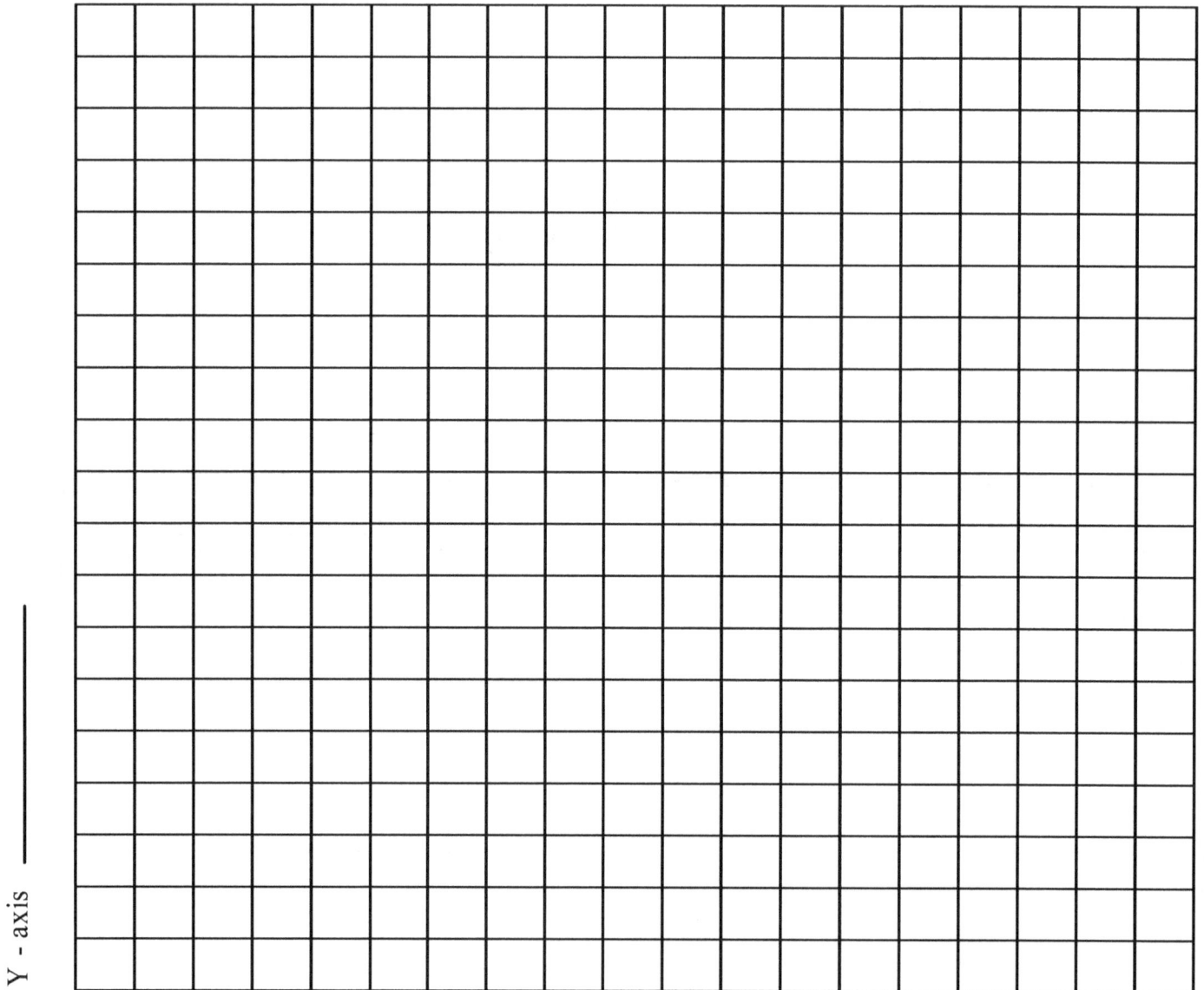

Y - axis

X - axis _____

(Hint - X-axis count by 5's
   Y-axis count by 10's)

Estimated ordered pair of intersection point

(,   )

In the space provided at the bottom of the page, set up the two equations below as a System of Equations and find the solution. Round solutions to the nearest hundredth place.

Pg. 177 Original Equation:

Pg. 181 Perpendicular Equation:

Solution:

Elaborate on the context of your solution above._____

_____

_____

Type the two equations below into the "y =" button on your calculator.

Pg. 177 Original Equation (Y_1):

Pg. 181 Perpendicular Equation (Y_2):

Original Equation		**Calculator Window**	**Perpendicular Equation**	
(Use coordinates from Pg. 177)			(Use coordinates from Pg. 181)	

Calculator Window

Xmin =

Xmax =

Xscl =

Ymax =

Ymin =

Yscl =

Xres =

L_1	L_2

L_1	L_3

Once you have plugged in all the data above into your calculator select "GRAPH". You should see both sets of points with lines going through them. If you do not see them, be creative and find a way, if that does not work then ask me. Once you see both, select "2nd", then "TRACE". This will send you to "CALC" which sets up different components to solve for. Select "5" - Intersection (which is the solution to both graphs). Move your cursor near the intersection using the arrow keys and hit enter 3 times.

Write the solution rounded to the hundredths place below.

Solution:

My box to check off.

Differences in y-values:

Pg. 179 Parallel Equation using function notation (Type into Y_3):

s(30)

Using the notation above, write a question that needs to be solved.

_____

s(30) =

Below, show the work needed to find the solution.

Ordered Pair

(   )

My box to check off.

The x - Value in context_____.

The s(x) - Value in context _____.

Pg. 181 Perpendicular Equation using function notation (Type into Y_2):

s(x) = 120   x =

Using the notation above, write a question that needs to be solved.

_____

s(x) = 120   x =

Below, show the work needed to find the solution.

How close is your solution to the calculator's? Calculate the differences in x - values and y - values from pages 183 and 184 then write the findings below. **Find one when you are finished so that I can check this page off.**   Ordered Pair

(   )

Differences in x-values:

My box to check off.

The x - Value in context _____.

The s(x) - Value in context _____.

Ch 4.3

We have paid $10,000 for the car and ramp sets that you are using. The car and ramps together were $250. Each photogate was $850. Let X be the car and ramp price and Y be the price of the photogates. Round # of photogates to the most sensible ones place.

# of car and ramps (X)	Value of car and ramps	Funds left for photogates	# of photogates (Y)
0			
			$\frac{0}{\ } =$

From the first 4 rows of the table above, generate an equation to find the number of photogates purchased as a function of the number of car and ramps purchased.

_____

What does the x - intercept mean in context of the problem? (Write ordered pair)

_____

_____

What does the y - intercept mean in context of the problem? (Write ordered pair)

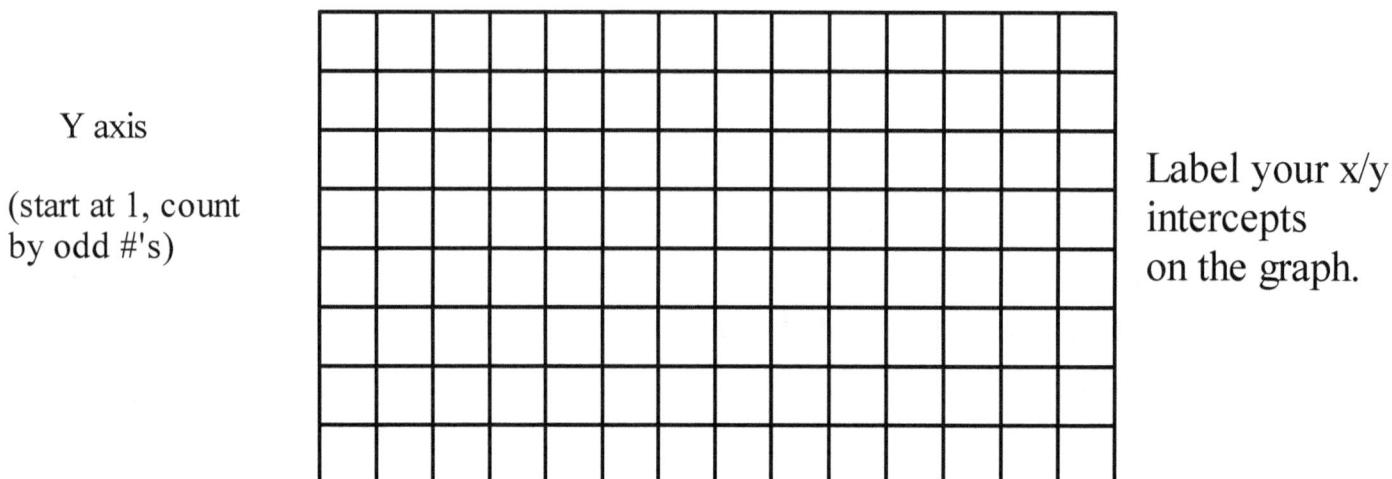

_____

Y axis

(start at 1, count by odd #'s)

Label your x/y intercepts on the graph.

X axis (count by 10's)

Take your data from the Slope Intercept equation at the bottom of Pg. 175 and do the following:

- Write your **Slope-Intercept Form** Answer from Pg. 175 below.

- **Graph** your equation using the **Y-Intercept** and **Slope** below.

Ch 4.5

Label your ordered pairs on the graph

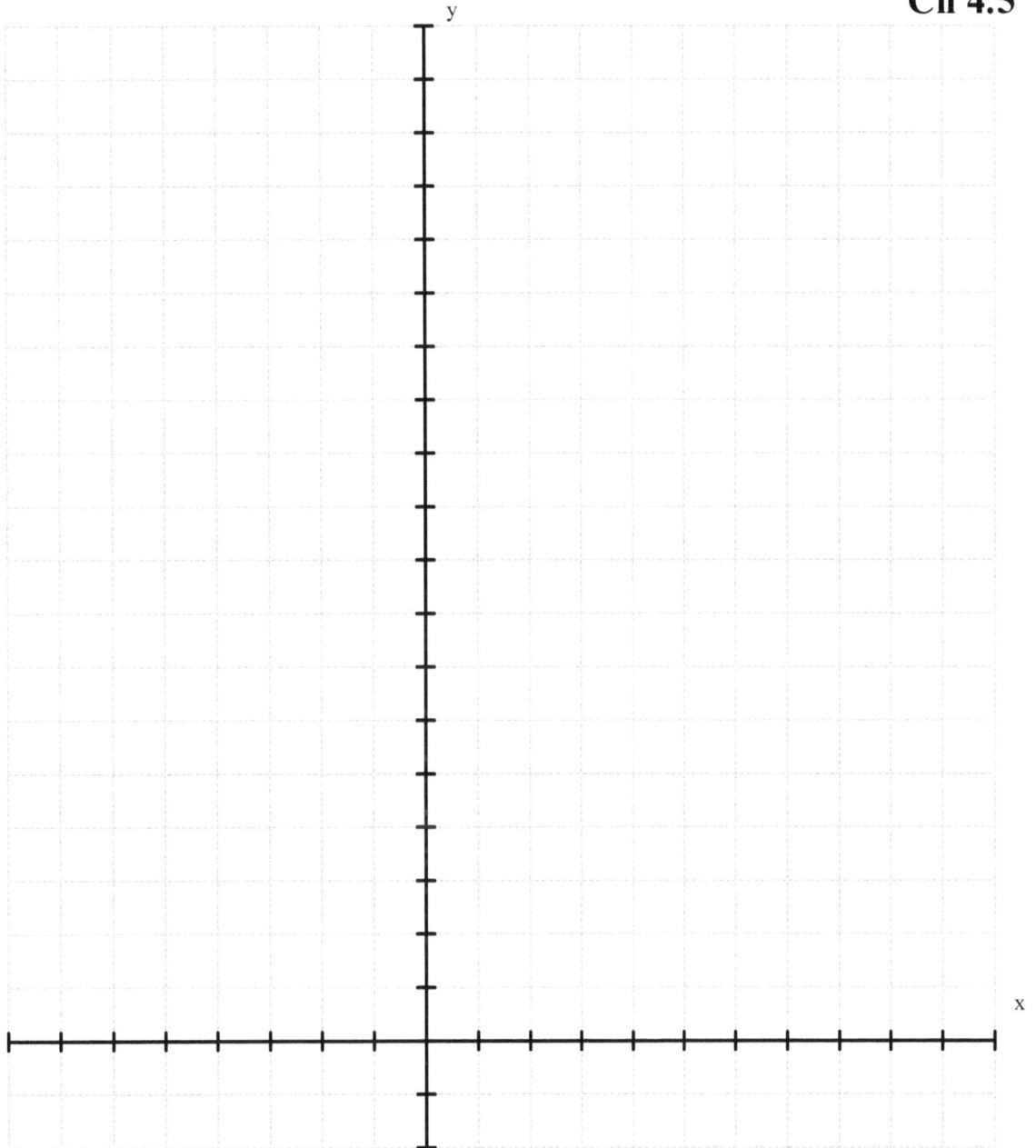

For your x and y axes, number them however you need to in order to **graph** at least 6 points. **Make sure you connect all possible points.**
List 6 consecutive ordered pairs below.

Pg.188

Blank page for additional space to show work, to write additional thoughts that come to mind, or to doodle if necessary.

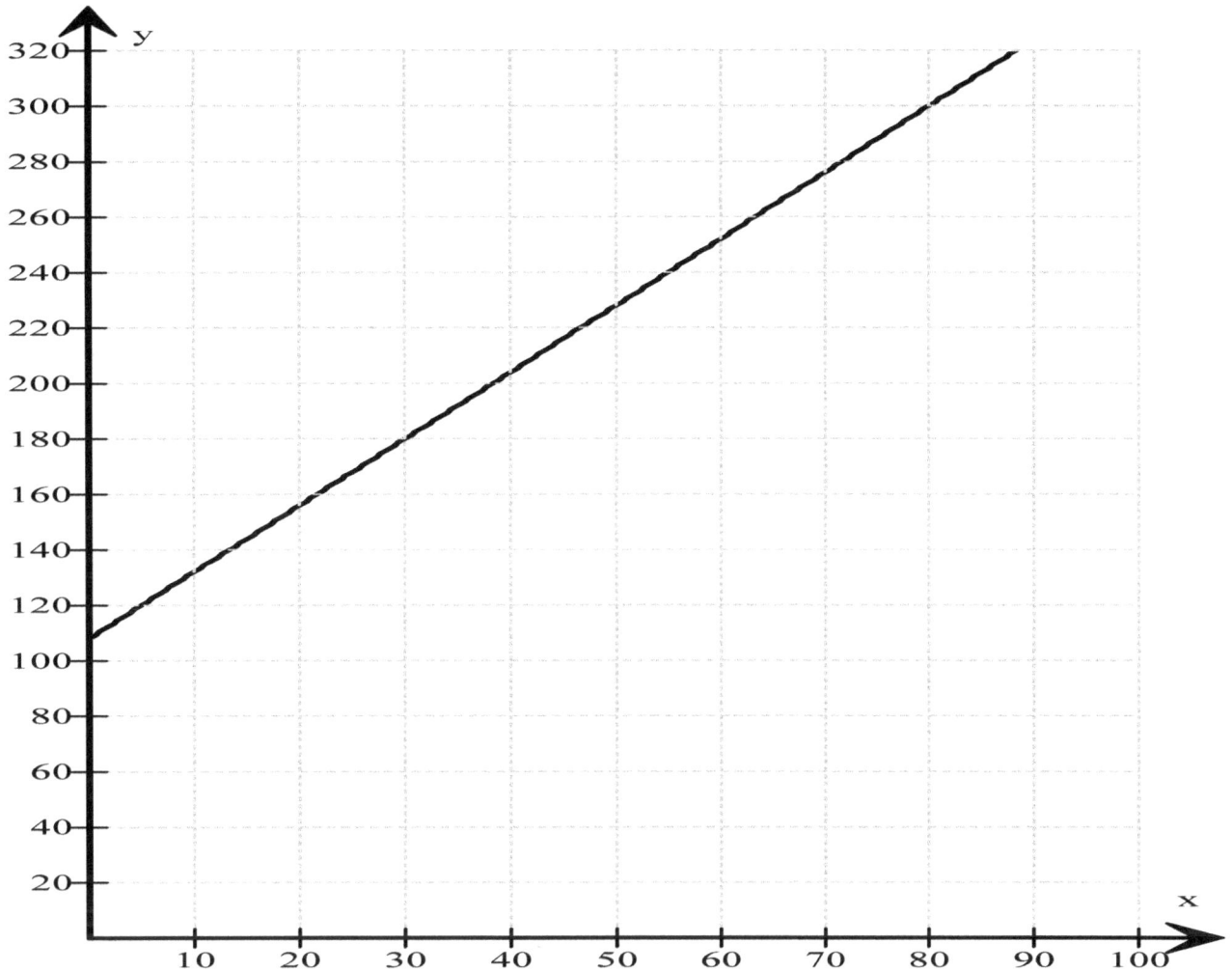

Use the graph above to answer questions 1 and 2. Use the words input and output when describing your solution in context.

1) s(40) = _____   Ordered Pair (   )

Write your total solution in context:_____

_____

2) s(x) ≈ 235 cm/s; x = _____   Ordered Pair (   )

Write your total solution in context:_____

_____

Grading Scales for all Chapters Covered in this Benchmark

- This is how I grade your benchmark. Do not worry about these pages until after I grade it.
- Refer to all scales previously passed out for each chapter to understand exactly what each score represents.
- Remember, there is No reason to guess in this classroom.

Chapter 1.6: Functions and Tables - Pg. 174

4	3.5	3	2.5	2	1.5	1

Chapter 4.1: Graphing on a Coordinate Plane - Pg. 174

4	3.5	3	2.5	2	1.5	1

Chapter 5.1: Slope Formula - Pg. 175

4	3.5	3	2.5	2	1.5	1

Chapter 5.2/5.3: Slope Intercept Form - Pg. 175

4	3.5	3	2.5	2	1.5	1

S.ID. 8: Linear Regression Using Technology - Pg. 176

4	3.5	3	2.5	2	1.5	1

Chapter 4.2: Graphing Linear Equations from Data - Pg. 177 & 178

4	3.5	3	2.5	2	1.5	1

Pg. 191

Chapter 5.5: Write and Graph Equations of Parallel Lines - Pg. 179 & 180

4	3.5	3	2.5	2	1.5	1

Chapter 5.5: Write/Graph Equations of Perpendicular Lines - Pg. 181 & 182

4	3.5	3	2.5	2	1.5	1

Chapter 7.2: Solving Linear Systems - Pg. 183 & 184

4	3.5	3	2.5	2	1.5	1

Chapter 4.7: Function Notation (Application) - Pg. 185 & 189

4	3.5	3	2.5	2	1.5	1

Chapter 4.3: X and Y Intercepts in Context - Pg. 186

4	3.5	3	2.5	2	1.5	1

Chapter 4.5: Graphing in Slope and Y-intercept Form - Pg. 187

4	3.5	3	2.5	2	1.5	1

Pg. 192   Car and Ramp Benchmark Individual Assessment Scenario 2

Position of Ramp	Position of Photogate *(X-Coordinate)*	Distance Traveled	2 Time Trials	Average Time Photogate	Speed of the car in "cm/s" *(Y-Coordinate)*
Hole 9	40				
Hole 9	50				
Hole 9	60				
Hole 9	70				

(Ch 1.6)

Label both your X and Y axes (same as the example)

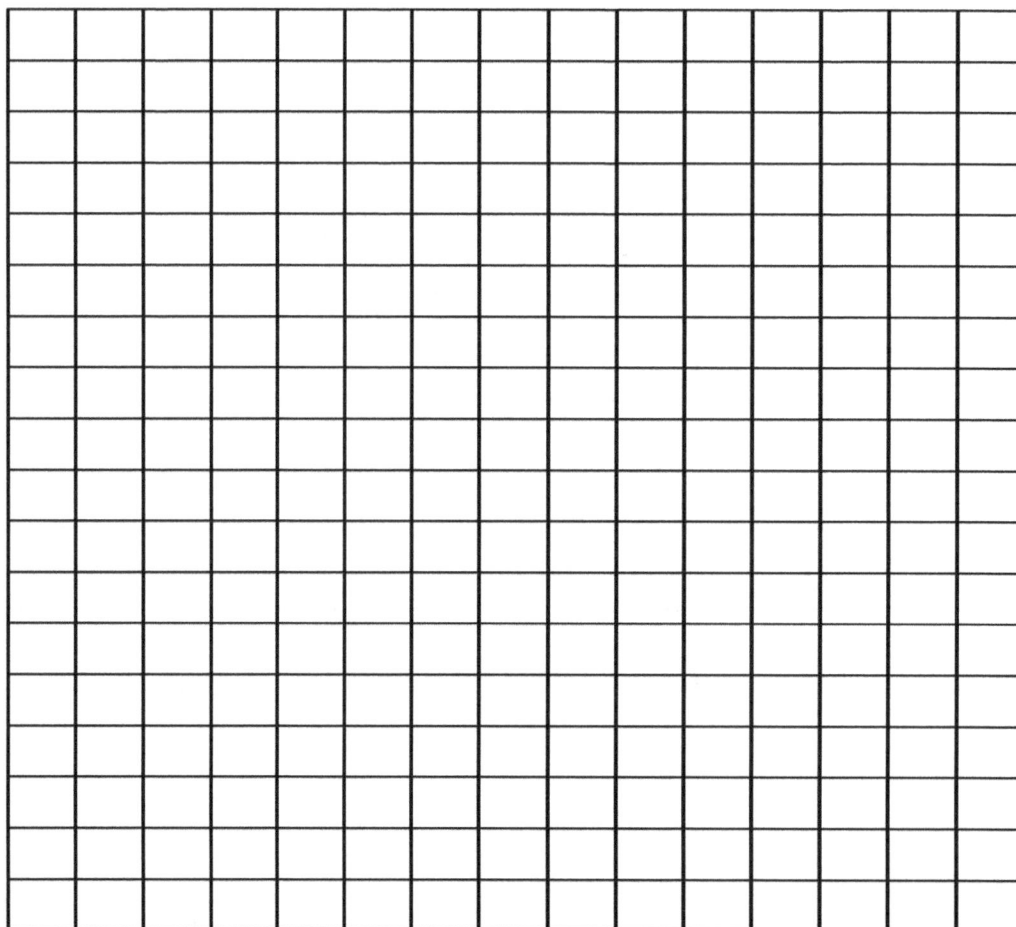

(Ch 4.1)

Y - axis (count by 20's)

Y - axis _____

Label your ordered pairs on the graph

X - axis _____   X - axis (Count by 5's)

(Chapter 5.1) Using the table on the previous page, <u>**derive the slope**</u>. <u>**Show all work below and place your answer in the box**</u>.

Slope (m) =

(Chapter 5.2/5.3) Using the slope above, formulate an equation in <u>**Slope-Intercept form.**</u> Show all work below and place your answer in the box.

Slope-Intercept form Answer using function notation (Ch 4.7):

Line of Best Fit (Linear Regression) Using Technology (S.ID.8)

L$_1$	L$_2$

Calculator Window

Xmin =   Xscl =   Ymax =   Xres =

Xmax =   Ymin =   Yscl =

Line of Best Fit/Linear Regression
(Write Linear Regression Equation below (for y)
subsituting values)
a =

b =

y =

r =

In the space to the below, elaborate on the **relationship** between the numerical value of the correlation coefficient and what it means in context to your data.

_____

_____

_____

Push the "Y=" button now plug the equation you derived from the slope-intercept form on the bottom of Pg. 193 into the calculator for (Y$_2$). Once that is completed push the "graph" button to compare **your** equation versus the **calculator's** linear regression. **Find me when finished to be checked off.**

My box to check off.

Directions - Generate an equation based on the data below.
Photogate at 40 cm and Speed at 99 cm/s. Photogate at 50 cm and Speed at 111 cm/s.
- Show mathematical work below.

Original Equation using function notation Ch 5.5:

(Domain - Start from 0 and Count by 15's)
(Range - Round to the ones place)

Use the equation above
to complete the table below.

Domain	Function	Range

Graph the equation from Pg. 195 on the coordinate plane below.

Label your ordered pairs on the graph.

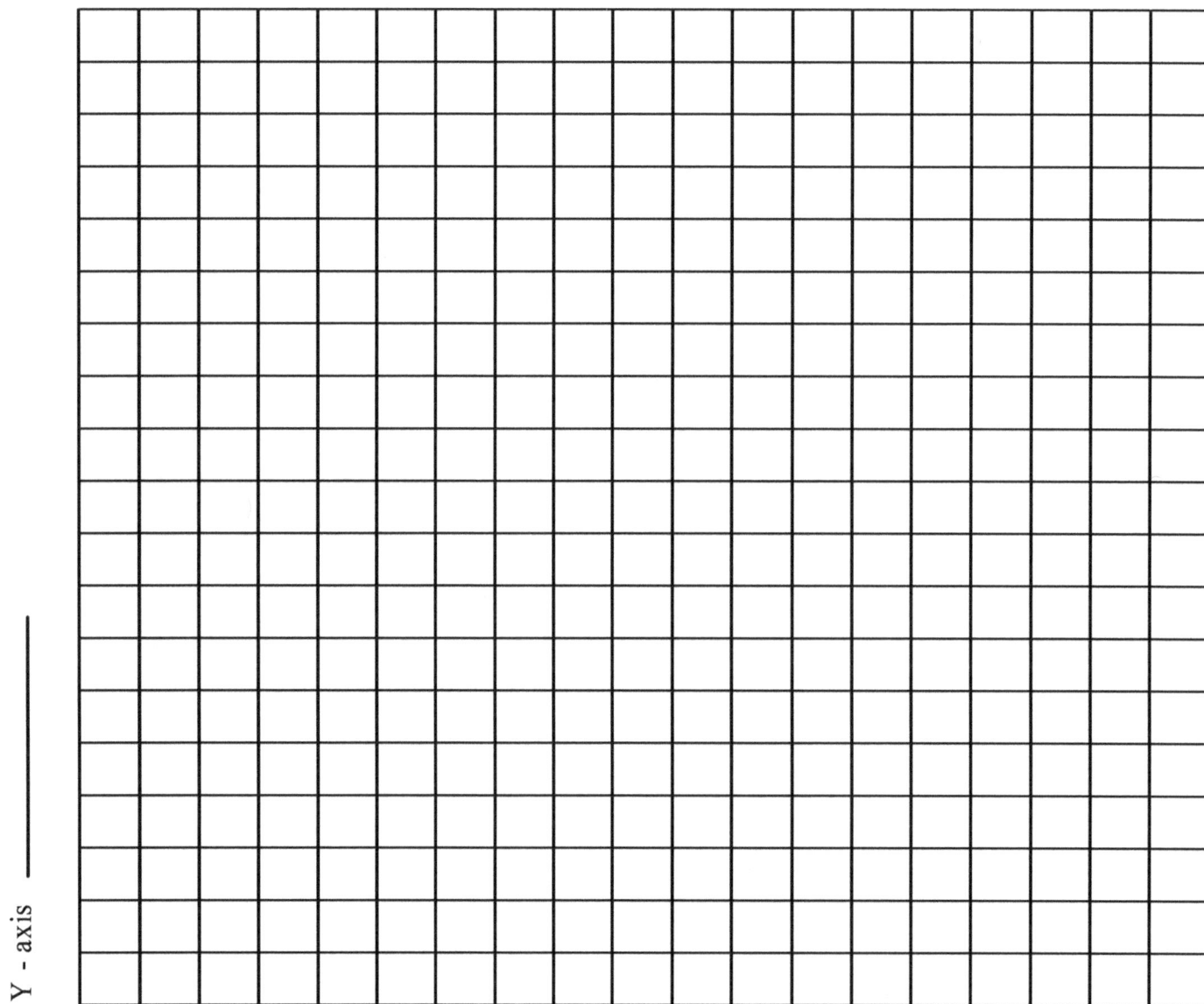

Y - axis

X - axis _____

(Hint - X-axis count by 5's
        Y-axis count by 10's)

Directions - Generate an equation **Parallel** to the one given to you on Pg. 195 that goes through a point with Photogate at 20 cm and Speed at 160 cm/s. **(Ch 5.5)** - **Show mathematical work below.**

Parallel Line Equation using function notation Ch 5.5:

(Write in words below how you <u>know</u> your line is <u>parallel.</u>

(Domain - Start from 0 and Count by 15's)
(Range - Round to the ones place)

Use the parallel equation above to complete the table below.

Domain	Function	Range

Pg. 198

First, graph the equation from Pg. 195 **again** on the coordinate plane below. Then, **Graph** the **parallel line equation** on the same coordinate plane using the **3 column table on the previous page.**

Label your ordered pairs on the graph.

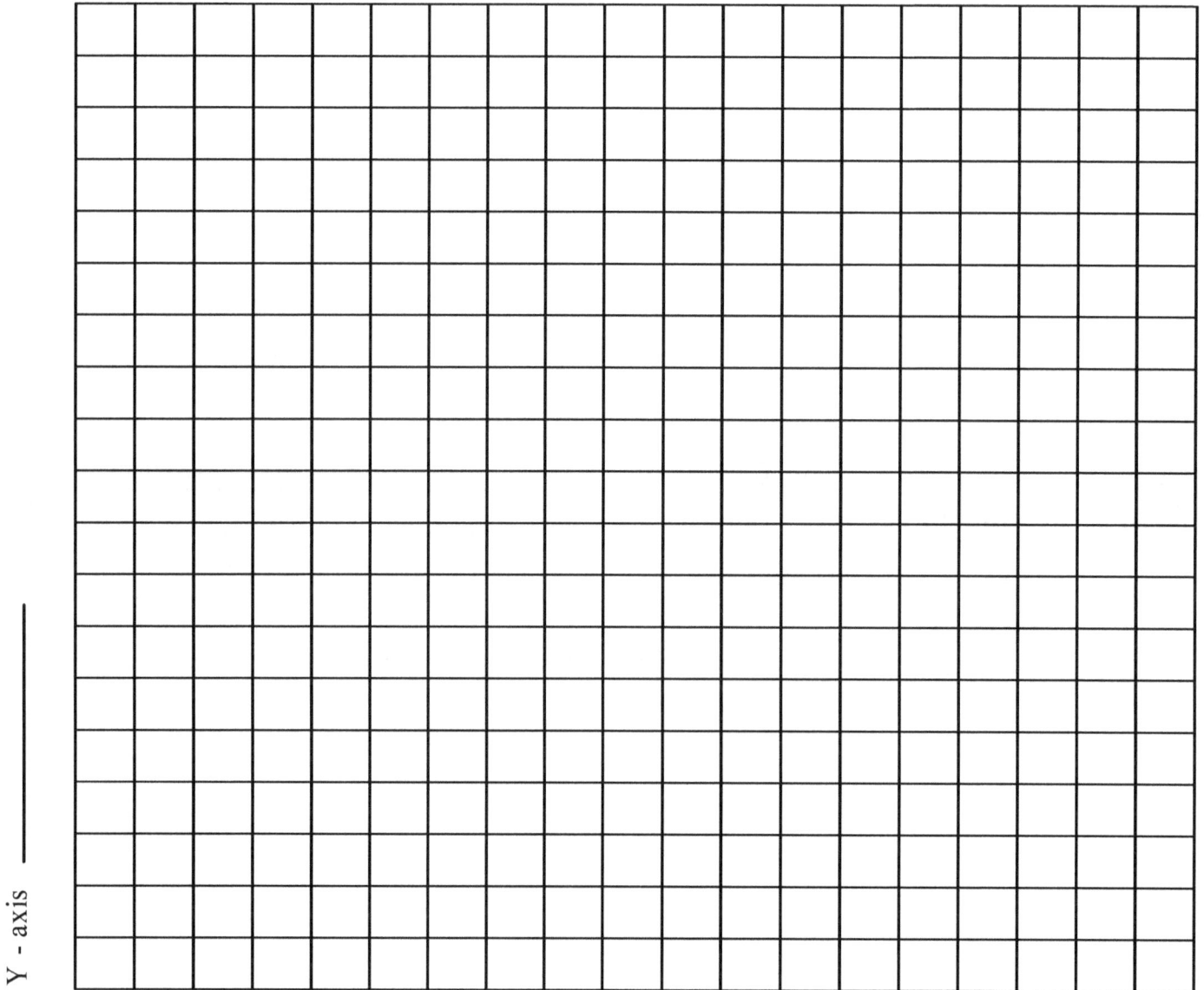

Y - axis _____

X - axis _____

(Hint - X-axis count by 5's
**   Y-axis count by 10's)**

Directions - Generate an equation **Perpendicular** to the one given to you on Pg. 195 that goes through a point with photogate at 90 cm and speed at 40 cm/s. **(Ch 5.5)**
- **Show mathematical work below.**

Perpendicular Line Equation using function notation Ch 5.5:

(**Write in words below how you know your line is perpendicular** - Also, what is the **product** of their slopes).

(Domain - Start from 0 and Count by 15's)
(Range - Round to the ones place)

Use the perpendicular equation above to complete the table below.

Domain	Function	Range

Pg. 200

First, graph the equation from Pg. 195 **again** on the coordinate plane below. Then,
Graph the **perpendicular line equation** on the same coordinate plane using the
3 column table on the previous page.

Label your ordered pairs on the graph (estimate the intersection point)

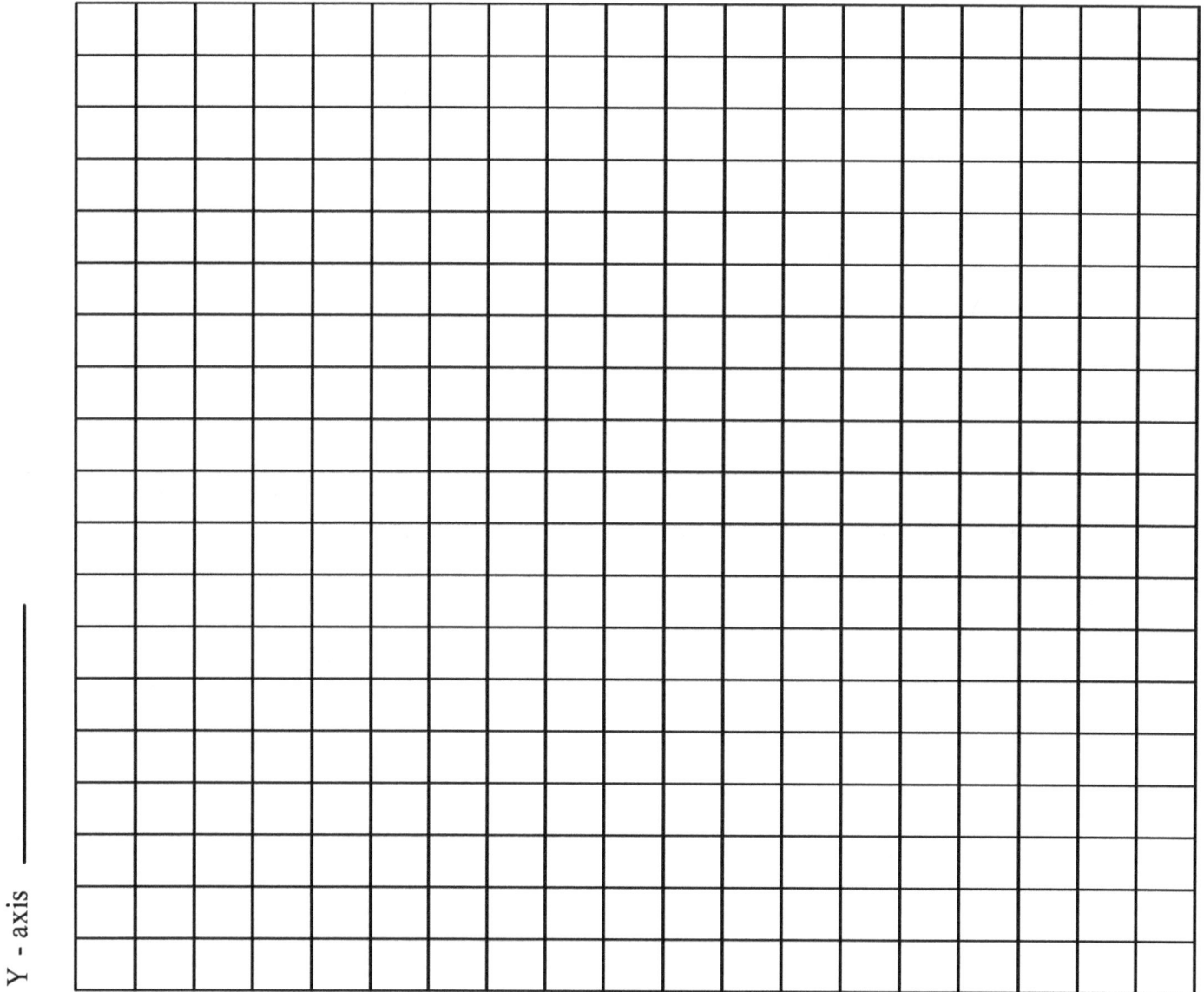

Y - axis

X - axis _____

(Hint - X-axis count by 5's
Y-axis count by 20's)

Estimated ordered pair of intersection point

(,   )

In the space provided at the bottom of the page, set up the two equations below as a System of Equations and find the solution. Round solutions to the nearest hundredth place.

Pg. 195 Original Equation:

Pg. 199 Perpendicular Equation:

Solution:

Elaborate on the context of your solution above._____

_____

_____

Using Technology to Aid With Solving Systems of Equations

Type the two equations below into the "y =" button on your calculator.

Pg. 195 Original Equation (Y_1):

Pg. 199 Perpendicular Equation (Y_2):

| **Original Equation** (Use coordinates from Pg. 195) | **Calculator Window** | **Perpendicular Equation** (Use coordinates from Pg. 199) |

L_1	L_2

Calculator Window

Xmin =

Xmax =

Xscl =

Ymax =

Ymin =

Yscl =

Xres =

L_1	L_3

Once you have plugged in all the data above into your calculator select "GRAPH". You should see both sets of points with lines going through them. If you do not see them, be creative and find a way, if that does not work then ask me. Once you see both, select "2nd", then "TRACE". This will send you to "CALC" which sets up different components to solve for. Select "5" - Intersection (which is the solution to both graphs). Move your cursor near the intersection using the arrow keys and hit enter 3 times.

Write the solution rounded to the hundredths place below.

Solution:

How close is your solution to the calculator's? Calculate the differences in x - values and y - values from pages 201 and 202 then write the findings below. **Find me when you are finished so that I can check this page off.**

Differences in x-values:

My box to check off.

Differences in y-values:

Pg. 197 Parallel Equation using function notation (Type into Y₃):

s(107)

Using the notation above, write a question that needs to be solved.

_____

s(107) =

Below, show the work needed to find the solution.

Ordered Pair

(   )

My box to check off.

The x - Value in context _____.

The s(x) - Value in context_____.

Pg. 199 Perpendicular Equation using function notation (Type into Y₂):

s(x) = 60   x =

Using the notation above, write a question that needs to be solved.

_____

s(x) = 60   x =

Below, show the work needed to find the solution.

Ordered Pair

(   )

My box to check off.

The x - Value in context _____.

The s(x) - Value in context _____.

Ch 4.3

We have paid $5,000 for the car and ramp sets that you are using. The car and ramps together were $200. Each photogate was $650. Let X be the car and ramp price and Y be the price of the photogates. Round # of photogates to the most sensible ones place.

# of car and ramps (X)	Value of car and ramps	Funds left for photogates	# of photogates (Y)
0			
			$\frac{0}{-}$ =

From the first 4 rows of the table above, generate an equation to find the number of photogates purchased as a function of the number of car and ramps purchased.

_____

What does the x - intercept mean in context of the problem? (Write ordered pair)

_____

_____

What does the y - intercept mean in context of the problem? (Write ordered pair)

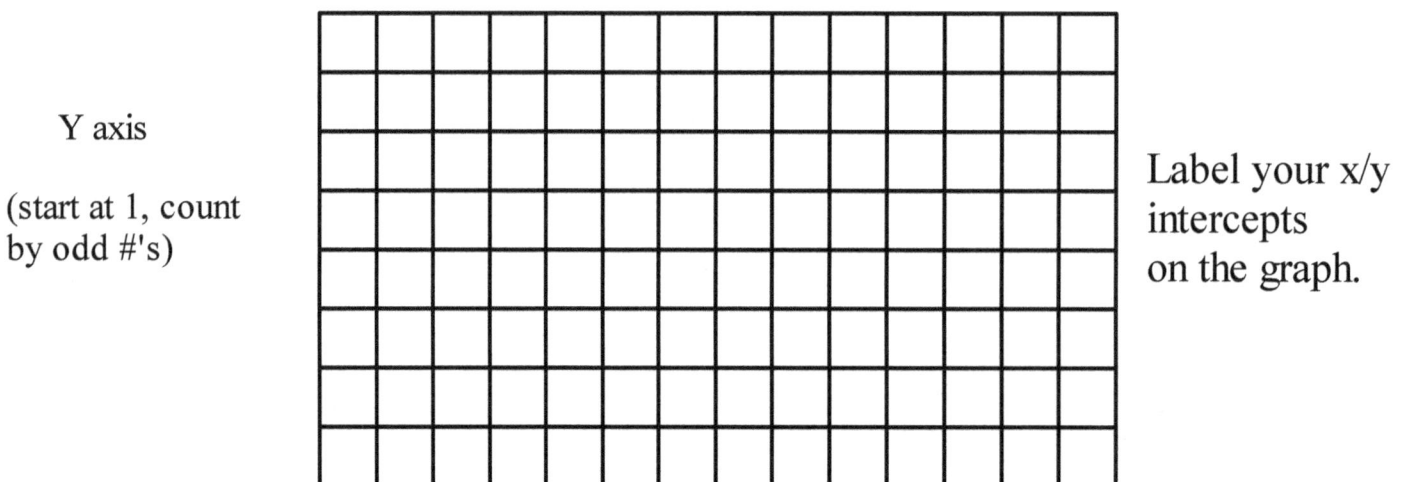

_____

Y axis

(start at 1, count by odd #'s)

Label your x/y intercepts on the graph.

X axis (count by 5's)

Take your data from the Slope Intercept equation at the bottom of Pg. 193 and do the following:

- Write your **Slope-Intercept Form** Answer from Pg. 193 below.

- **Graph** your equation using the **Y-Intercept** and **Slope** below.

Ch 4.5

Label your ordered pairs on the graph

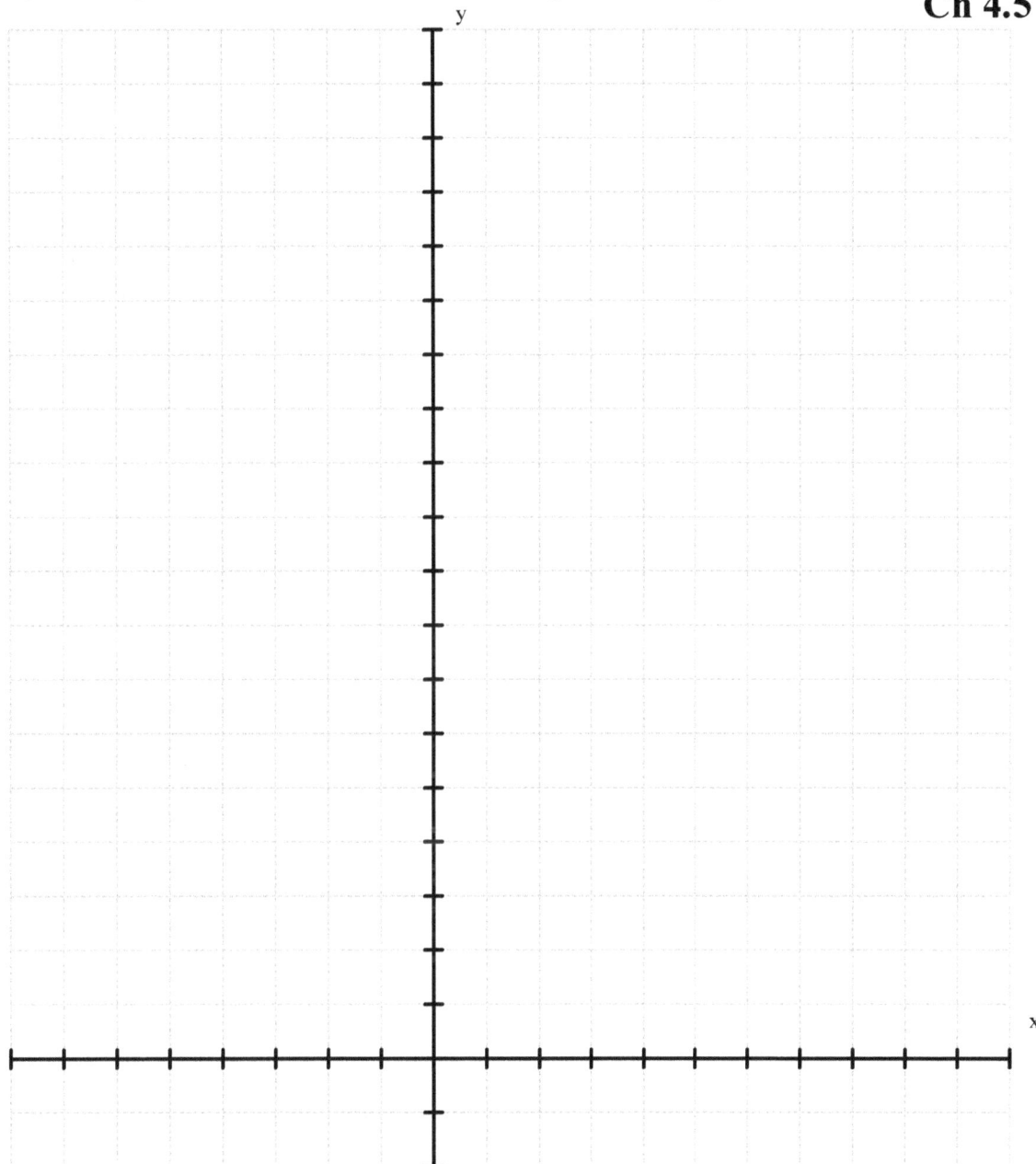

For your x and y axes, number them however you need to in order to **graph** at least 6 points. **Make sure you connect all possible points.**

List 6 consecutive ordered pairs below.

Pg.206

Blank page for additional space to show work, to write additional thoughts that come to mind, or to doodle if necessary.

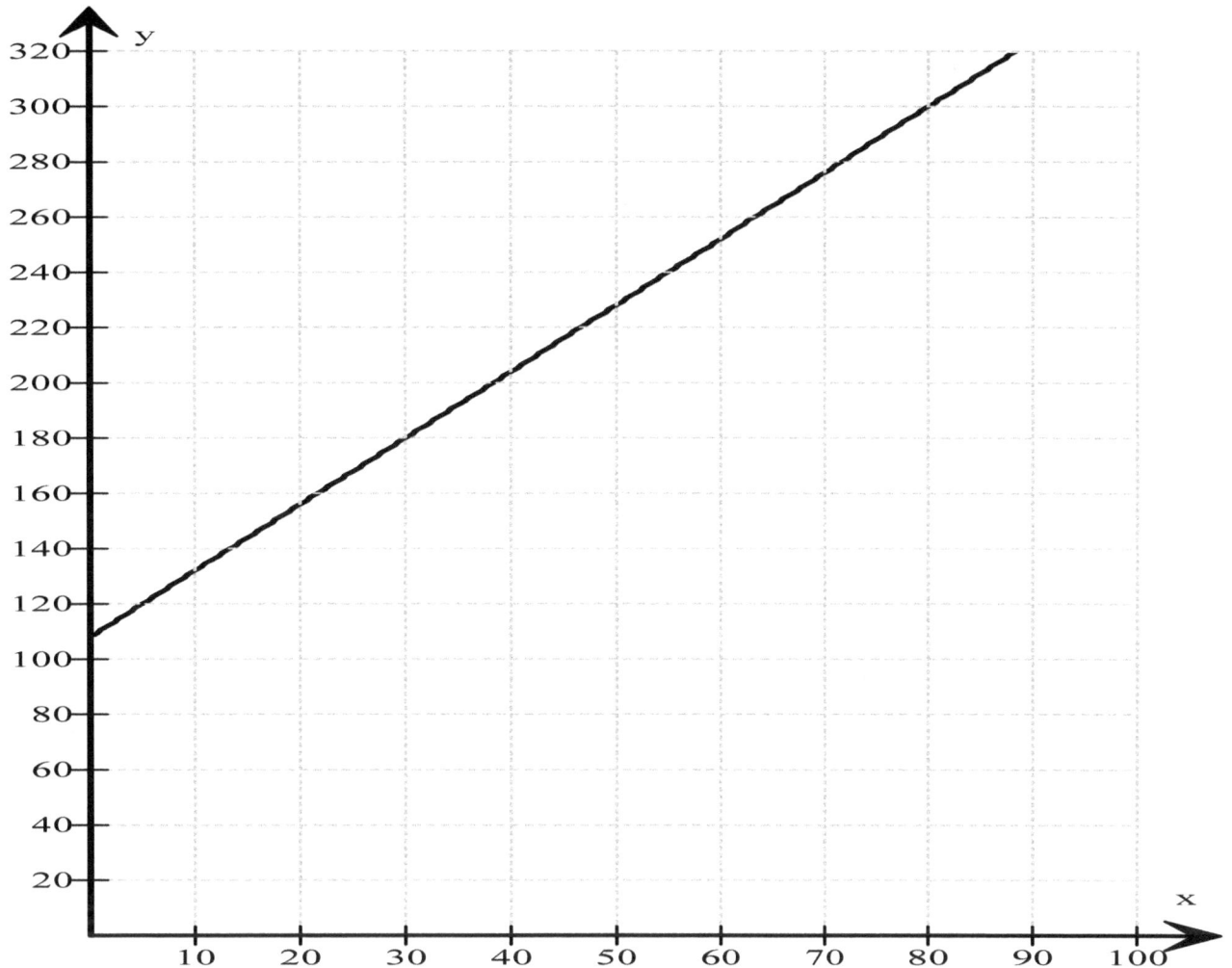

Use the graph above to answer questions 1 and 2. Use the words input and output when describing your solution in context.

1) s(70) = _____   Ordered Pair (   )

Write your total solution in context:_____

_____

2) s(x) ≈ 280 cm/s; x = _____   Ordered Pair (   )

Write your total solution in context:_____

_____

Grading Scales for all Chapters Covered in this Benchmark

- This is how I grade your benchmark. Do not worry about these pages until after I grade it.
*- Refer to **all** scales **previously** passed out for each chapter to understand **exactly** what each score represents.*
*- Remember, there is **No** reason to guess in this classroom.*

Chapter 1.6: Functions and Tables - Pg. 192

4	3.5	3	2.5	2	1.5	1

Chapter 4.1: Graphing on a Coordinate Plane - Pg. 192

4	3.5	3	2.5	2	1.5	1

Chapter 5.1: Slope Formula - Pg. 193

4	3.5	3	2.5	2	1.5	1

Chapter 5.2/5.3: Slope Intercept Form - Pg. 193

4	3.5	3	2.5	2	1.5	1

S.ID. 8: Linear Regression Using Technology - Pg. 194

4	3.5	3	2.5	2	1.5	1

Chapter 4.2: Graphing Linear Equations from Data - Pg. 195 & 196

4	3.5	3	2.5	2	1.5	1

Chapter 5.5: Write and Graph Equations of Parallel Lines - Pg. 197 & 198

4	3.5	3	2.5	2	1.5	1

Chapter 5.5: Write/Graph Equations of Perpendicular Lines - Pg. 199 & 200

4	3.5	3	2.5	2	1.5	1

Chapter 7.2: Solving Linear Systems - Pg. 201 & 202

4	3.5	3	2.5	2	1.5	1

Chapter 4.7: Function Notation (Application) - Pg. 203 & 207

4	3.5	3	2.5	2	1.5	1

Chapter 4.3: X and Y Intercepts in Context - Pg. 204

4	3.5	3	2.5	2	1.5	1

Chapter 4.5: Graphing in Slope and Y-intercept Form - Pg. 205

4	3.5	3	2.5	2	1.5	1

Car and Ramp Benchmark Individual Assessment Scenario 3

Position of Ramp	Position of Photogate (X-Coordinate)	Distance Traveled	2 Time Trials	Average Time Photogate	Speed of the car in "cm/s" (Y-Coordinate)
Hole 15	40				
Hole 15	50				
Hole 15	60				
Hole 15	70				

(Ch 1.6)

Label both your X and Y axes (same as the example)

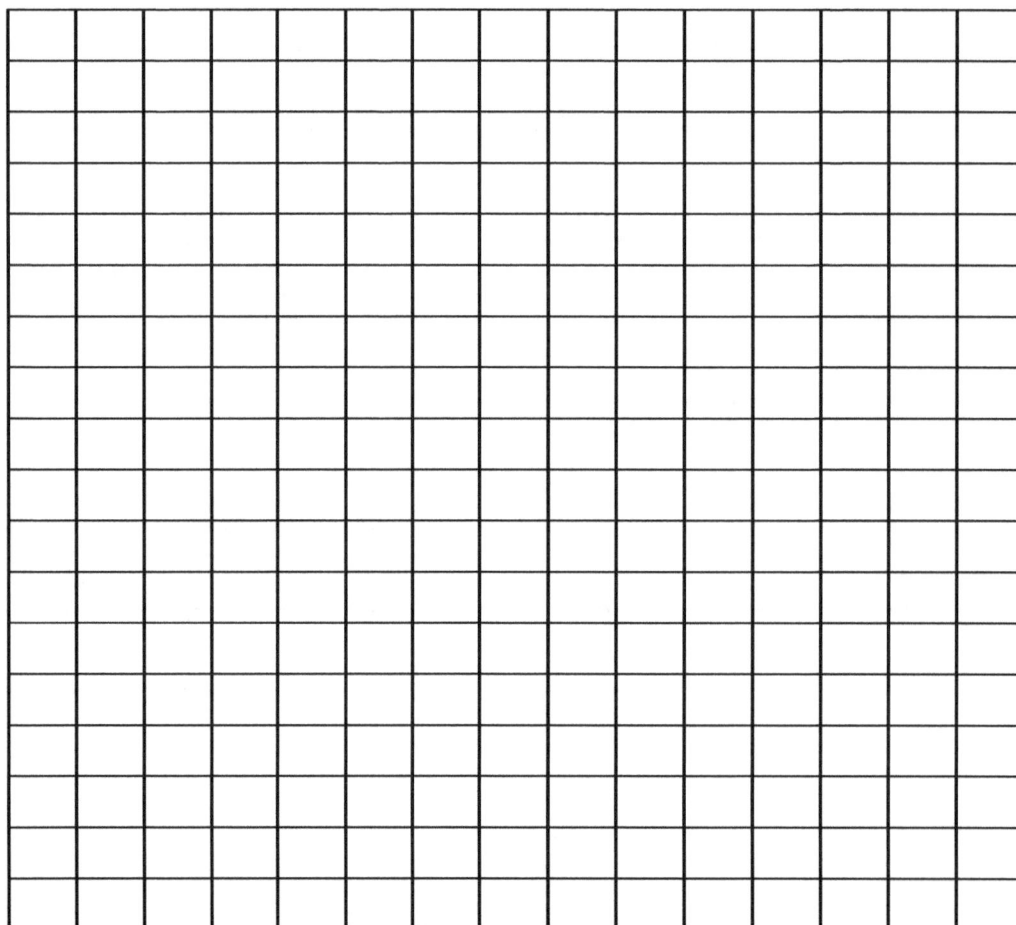

(Ch 4.1)

Y - axis (count by 20's)

Y - axis

Label your ordered pairs on the graph

X - axis _____   X - axis (Count by 5's)

(Chapter 5.1) Using the table on the previous page, **derive the slope**. **Show all work below and place your answer in the box**.

Slope (m) =

(Chapter 5.2/5.3) Using the slope above, formulate an equation in **Slope-Intercept form.** Show all work below and place your answer in the box.

Slope-Intercept form Answer using function notation (Ch 4.7):

Pg. 212   **Line of Best Fit (Linear Regression) Using Technology (S.ID.8)**

L_1	L_2

Calculator Window

Xmin =   Xscl =   Ymax =   Xres =

Xmax =   Ymin =   Yscl =

Line of Best Fit/Linear Regression
(Write Linear Regression Equation below (for y)
subsituting values)
a =

b =

y =

r =

In the space to the below, elaborate on the **relationship** between the numerical value of the correlation coefficient and what it means in context to your data.

_____

_____

_____

Push the "Y=" button now plug the equation you derived from the slope-intercept form on the bottom of Pg. 211 into the calculator for (Y_2). Once that is completed push the "graph" button to compare **your** equation versus the **calculator's** linear regression. **Find me when finished to be checked off.**

My box to check off.

Directions - Generate an equation based on the data below.
Photogate at 40 cm and Speed at 150 cm/s. Photogate at 50 cm and Speed at 167 cm/s.
- **Show mathematical work below.**

Original Equation using function notation Ch 5.5:

(Domain - Start from 0 and Count by 15's)
(Range - Round to the ones place)

Use the equation above
to complete the table below.

Domain	Function	Range

Graph the equation from Pg. 213 on the coordinate plane below.

Label your ordered pairs on the graph.

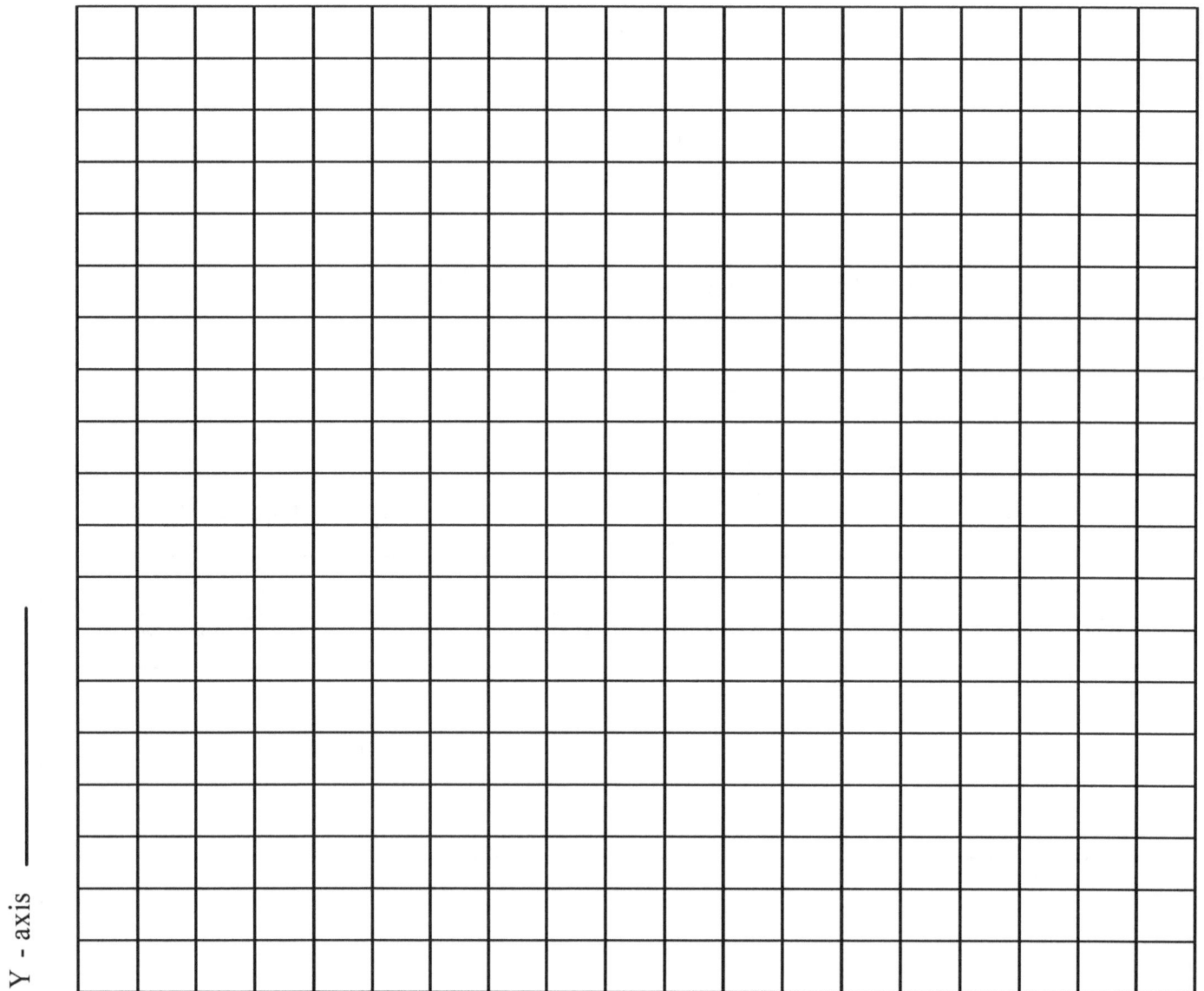

Y - axis

X - axis _____

**(Hint - X-axis count by 5's
Y-axis count by 10's)**

Directions - Generate an equation **Parallel** to the one given to you on Pg. 213 that goes through a point with Photogate at 10 cm and Speed at 130 cm/s. **(Ch 5.5)**
- **Show mathematical work below.**

Parallel Line Equation using function notation Ch 5.5:

(Write in words below how you **know** your line is **parallel.**

(Domain - Start from 0 and Count by 15's)   *Use the parallel equation*
(Range - Round to the ones place)   *above to complete the table below.*

Domain	Function	Range

Pg. 216

First, graph the equation from Pg. 213 **again** on the coordinate plane below. Then, **Graph** the **parallel line equation** on the same coordinate plane using the **3 column table on the previous page.**

Label your ordered pairs on the graph.

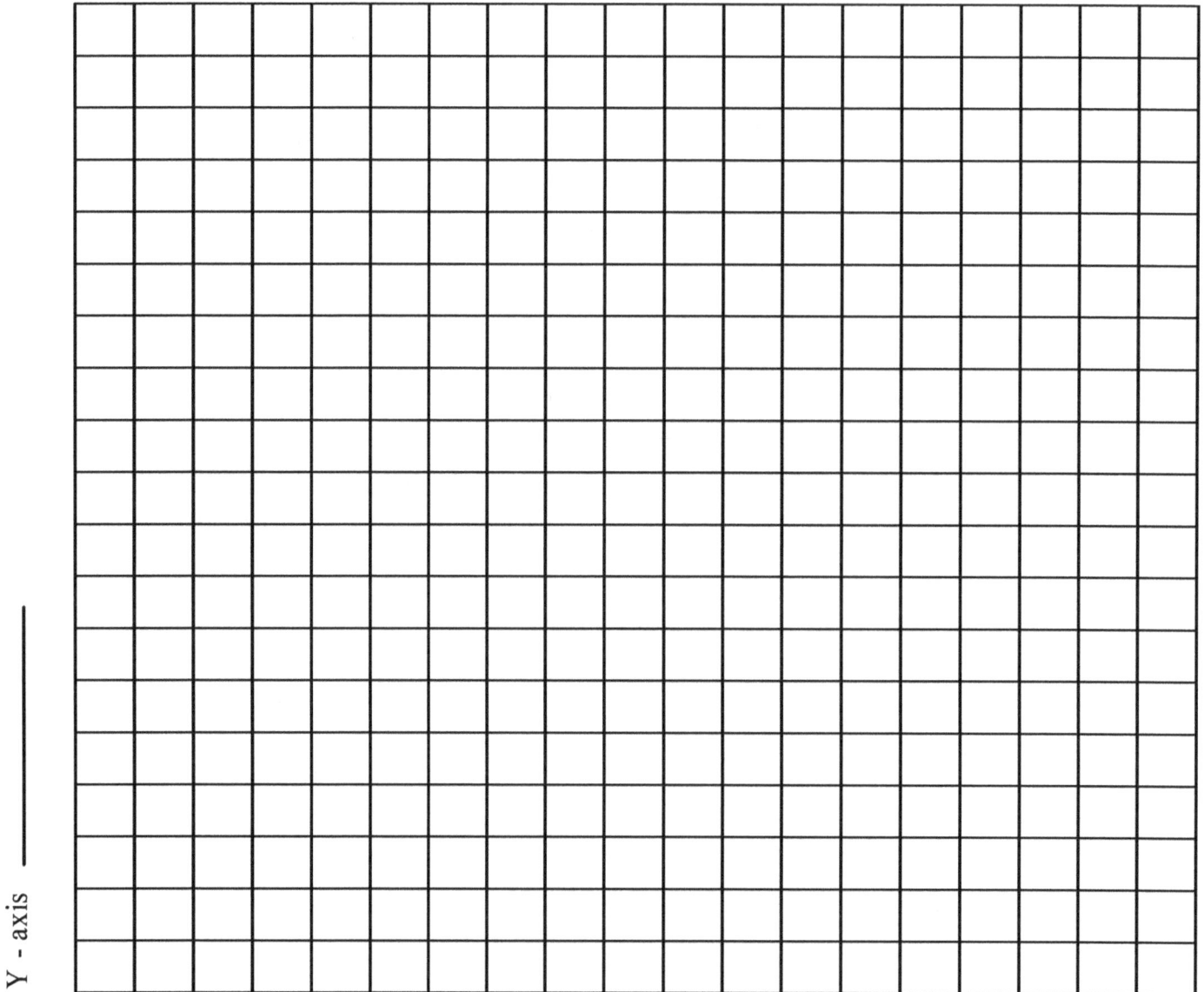

Y - axis

X - axis _____

(Hint - X-axis count by 5's
Y-axis count by 10's)

Directions - Generate an equation **Perpendicular** to the one given to you on Pg. 213 that goes through a point with photogate at 60 cm and speed at 100 cm/s. **(Ch 5.5)**
- Show mathematical work below.

Perpendicular Line Equation using function notation Ch 5.5:

(Write in words below how you <u>know</u> your line is <u>perpendicular</u> - Also, what is the **product** of their slopes).

(Domain - Start from 0 and Count by 15's)
(Range - Round to the ones place)

<u>Use the perpendicular equation</u>
<u>above to complete the table below.</u>

Domain	Function	Range

Pg. 218

First, graph the equation from Pg. 213 **again** on the coordinate plane below. Then,
Graph the **perpendicular line equation** on the same coordinate plane using the
3 column table on the previous page.

Label your ordered pairs on the graph (estimate the intersection point)

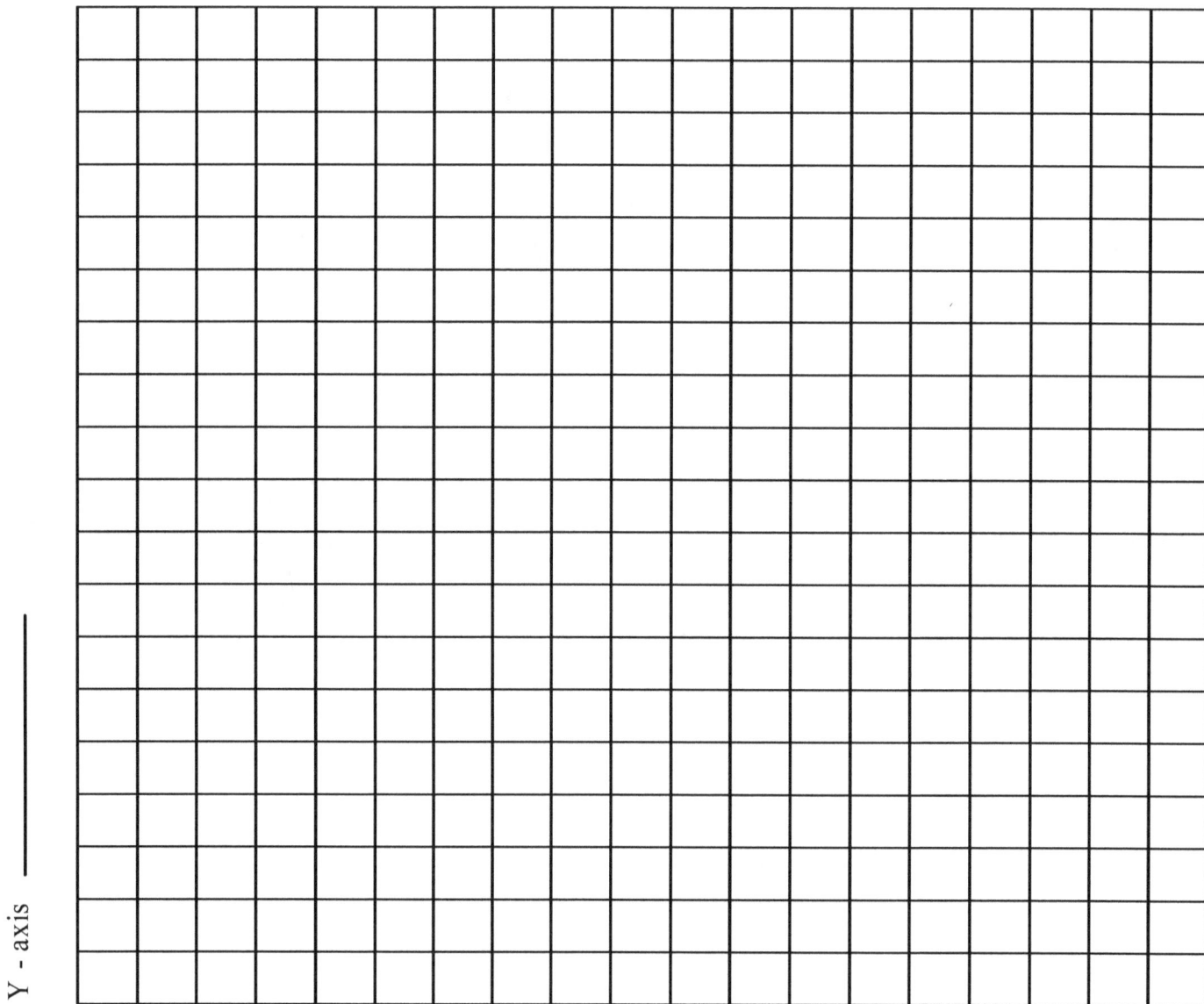

Y - axis

X - axis _____

(Hint - X-axis count by 5's
        Y-axis count by 20's)

Estimated ordered pair of intersection point

(,   )

In the space provided at the bottom of the page, set up the two equations below as a System of Equations and find the solution. Round solutions to the nearest hundredth place.

Pg. 213 Original Equation:

Pg. 217 Perpendicular Equation:

Solution:

Elaborate on the context of your solution above._____

_____

_____

Using Technology to Aid With Solving Systems of Equations

Type the two equations below into the "y =" button on your calculator.

Pg. 213 Original Equation (Y_1):

Pg. 217 Perpendicular Equation (Y_2):

Original Equation	**Calculator Window**	**Perpendicular Equation**
(Use coordinates from Pg. 213)		(Use coordinates from Pg. 217)

Original Equation
(Use coordinates from Pg. 213)

L_1	L_2

Calculator Window

Xmin =

Xmax =

Xscl =

Ymax =

Ymin =

Yscl =

Xres =

Perpendicular Equation
(Use coordinates from Pg. 217)

L_1	L_3

Once you have plugged in all the data above into your calculator select "GRAPH". You should see both sets of points with lines going through them. If you do not see them, be creative and find a way, if that does not work then ask me. Once you see both, select "2nd", then "TRACE". This will send you to "CALC" which sets up different components to solve for. Select "5" - Intersection (which is the solution to both graphs). Move your cursor near the intersection using the arrow keys and hit enter 3 times.

Write the solution rounded to the hundredths place below.

Solution:

How close is your solution to the calculator's? Calculate the differences in x - values and y - values from pages 219 and 220 then write the findings below. **Find me when you are finished so that I can check this page off.**

Differences in x-values:

My box to check off.

Differences in y-values:

Pg. 215 Parallel Equation using function notation (Type into Y₃):

s(65) =

Using the notation above, write a question that needs to be solved.

_____

s(65) =

Below, show the work needed to find the solution.

Ordered Pair

(   )

My box to check off.

The x - Value in context _____.

The s(x) - Value in context_____.

Pg. 217 Perpendicular Equation using function notation (Type into Y₂):

s(x) = 240   x =

Using the notation above, write a question that needs to be solved.

_____

s(x) = 240   x =

Below, show the work needed to find the solution.

Ordered Pair

(   )

My box to check off.

The x - Value in context _____.

The s(x) - Value in context _____.

Ch 4.3

We have paid $8,000 for the car and ramp sets that you are using. The car and ramps together were $400. Each photogate was $800. Let X be the car and ramp price and Y be the price of the photogates. Round # of photogates to the most sensible ones place.

# of car and ramps (X)	Value of car and ramps	Funds left for photogates	# of photogates (Y)
0			
			0 =

From the first 4 rows of the table above, generate an equation to find the number of photogates purchased as a function of the number of car and ramps purchased.

____

What does the x - intercept mean in context of the problem? (Write ordered pair)

____

____

What does the y - intercept mean in context of the problem? (Write ordered pair)

____

Y axis

(start at 2, count by odd #'s)

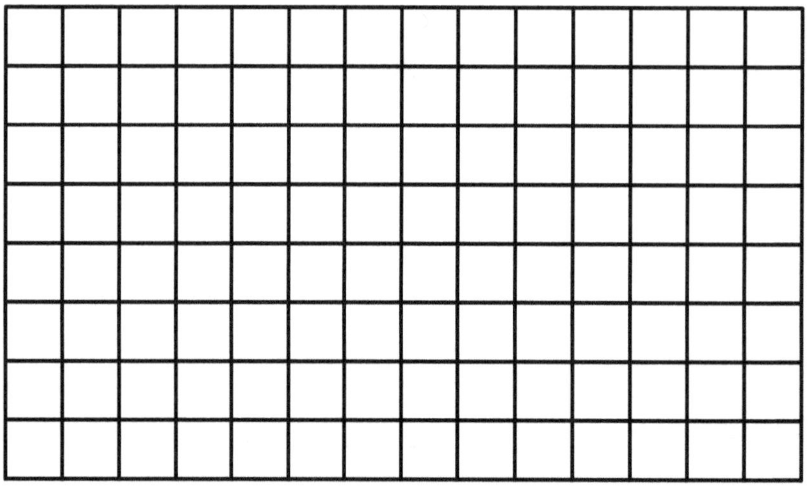

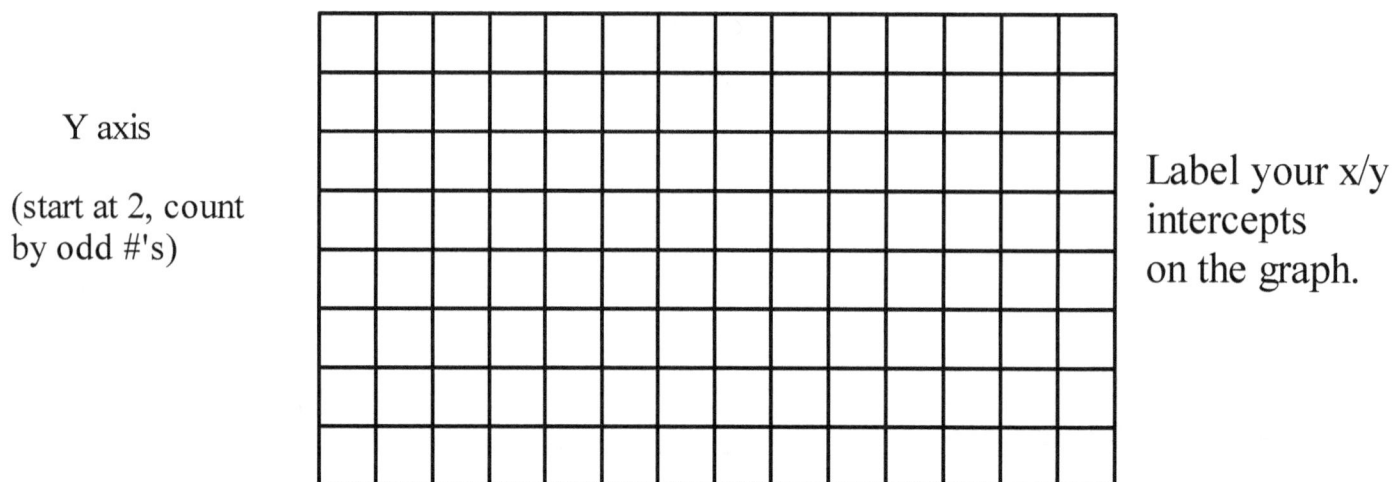

Label your x/y intercepts on the graph.

X axis (count by 2's)

Take your data from the Slope Intercept equation at the bottom of Pg. 211 and do the following:

- Write your **Slope-Intercept Form** Answer from Pg. 211 below.

- **Graph** your equation using the **Y-Intercept** and **Slope** below.

Ch 4.5

Label your ordered pairs on the graph

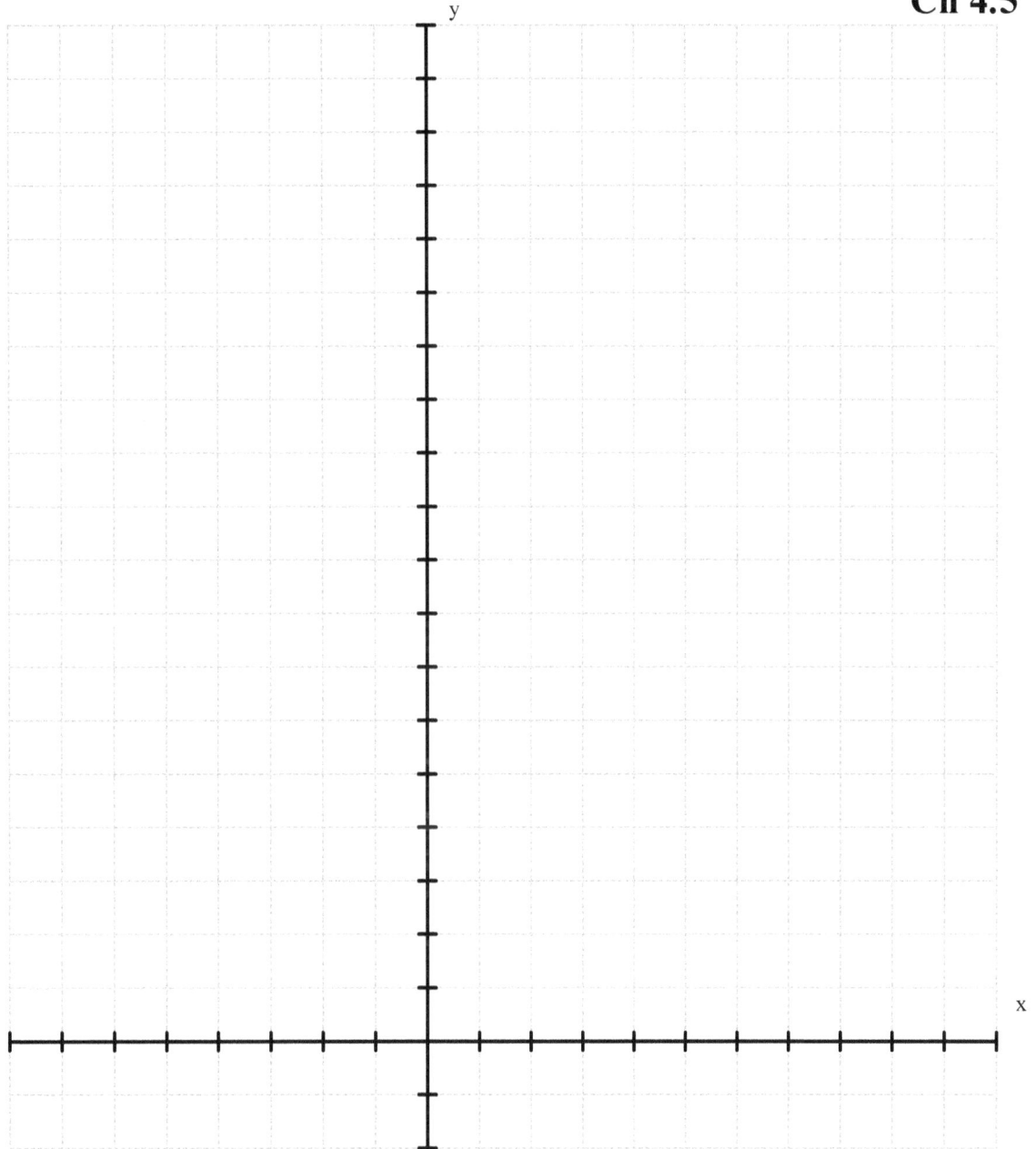

For your x and y axes, number them however you need to in order to **graph** at least 6 points. **Make sure you connect all possible points.**
List 6 consecutive ordered pairs below.

Blank page for additional space to show work, to write additional thoughts that come to mind, or to doodle if necessary.

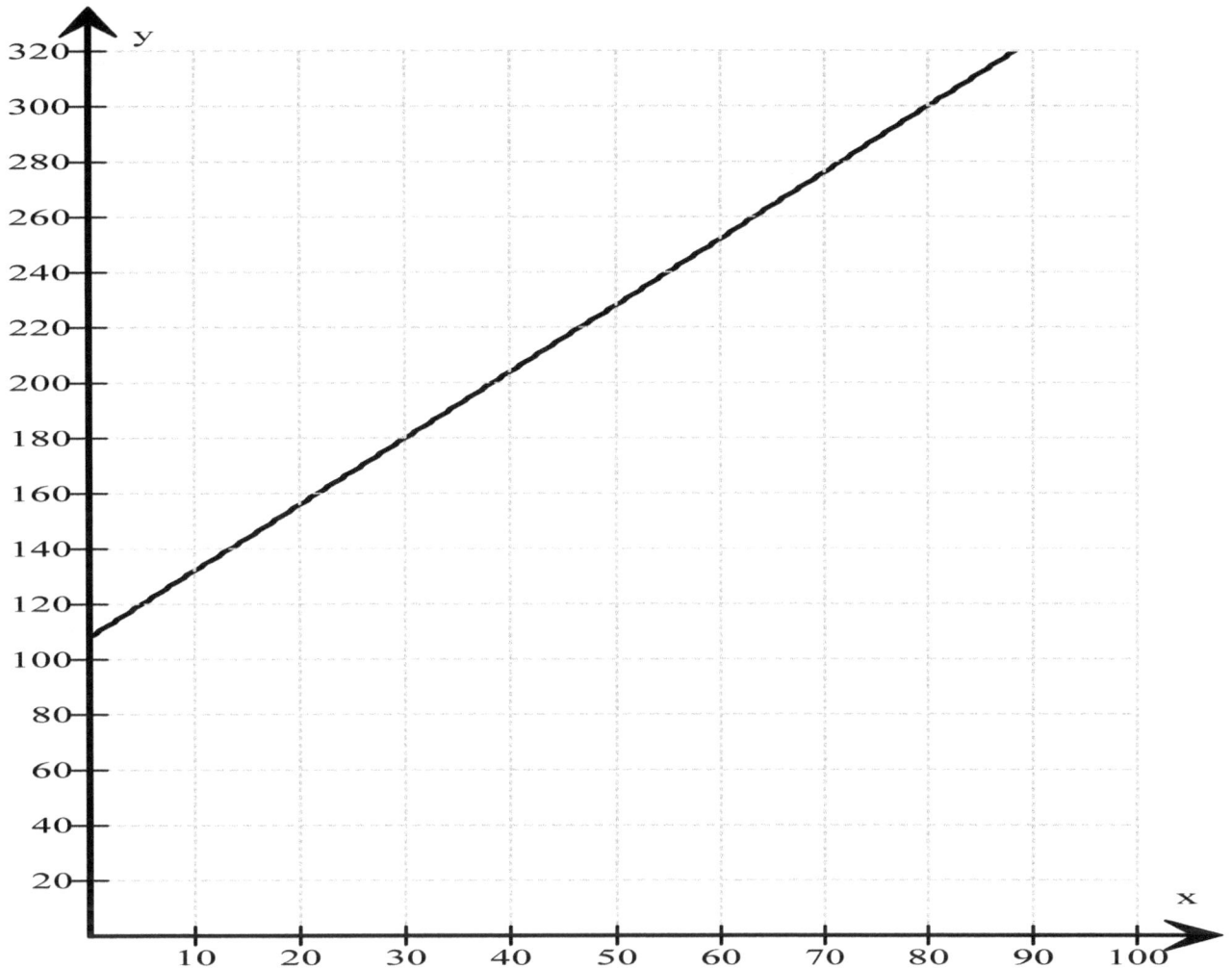

Use the graph above to answer questions 1 and 2. Use the words input and output when describing your solution in context.

1) s(50) = _____   Ordered Pair (   )

Write your total solution in context:_____

_____

2) s(x) ≈ 119 cm/s; x = _____   Ordered Pair (   )

Write your total solution in context:_____

_____

Grading Scales for all Chapters Covered in this Benchmark

- This is how I grade your benchmark. Do not worry about these pages until after I grade it.
- Refer to __all__ scales __previously__ passed out for each chapter to understand __exactly__ what each score represents.
- Remember, there is __No__ reason to guess in this classroom.

Chapter 1.6: Functions and Tables - Pg. 210

4	3.5	3	2.5	2	1.5	1

Chapter 4.1: Graphing on a Coordinate Plane - Pg. 210

4	3.5	3	2.5	2	1.5	1

Chapter 5.1: Slope Formula - Pg. 211

4	3.5	3	2.5	2	1.5	1

Chapter 5.2/5.3: Slope Intercept Form - Pg. 211

4	3.5	3	2.5	2	1.5	1

S.ID. 8: Linear Regression Using Technology - Pg. 212

4	3.5	3	2.5	2	1.5	1

Chapter 4.2: Graphing Linear Equations from Data - Pg. 213 & 214

4	3.5	3	2.5	2	1.5	1

Chapter 5.5: Write and Graph Equations of Parallel Lines - Pg. 215 & 216

4	3.5	3	2.5	2	1.5	1

Chapter 5.5: Write/Graph Equations of Perpendicular Lines - Pg. 217 & 218

4	3.5	3	2.5	2	1.5	1

Chapter 7.2: Solving Linear Systems - Pg. 219 & 220

4	3.5	3	2.5	2	1.5	1

Chapter 4.7: Function Notation (Application) - Pg. 221 & 225

4	3.5	3	2.5	2	1.5	1

Chapter 4.3: X and Y Intercepts in Context - Pg. 222

4	3.5	3	2.5	2	1.5	1

Chapter 4.5: Graphing in Slope and Y-intercept Form - Pg. 223

4	3.5	3	2.5	2	1.5	1

Pg. 228   Car and Ramp Benchmark Individual Assessment Scenario 4

Position of Ramp	Position of Photogate (X-Coordinate)	Distance Traveled	2 Time Trials	Average Time Photogate	Speed of the car in "cm/s" (Y-Coordinate)
Hole 5	40				
Hole 5	50				
Hole 5	60				
Hole 5	70				

(Ch 1.6)

Label both your X and Y axes (same as the example)

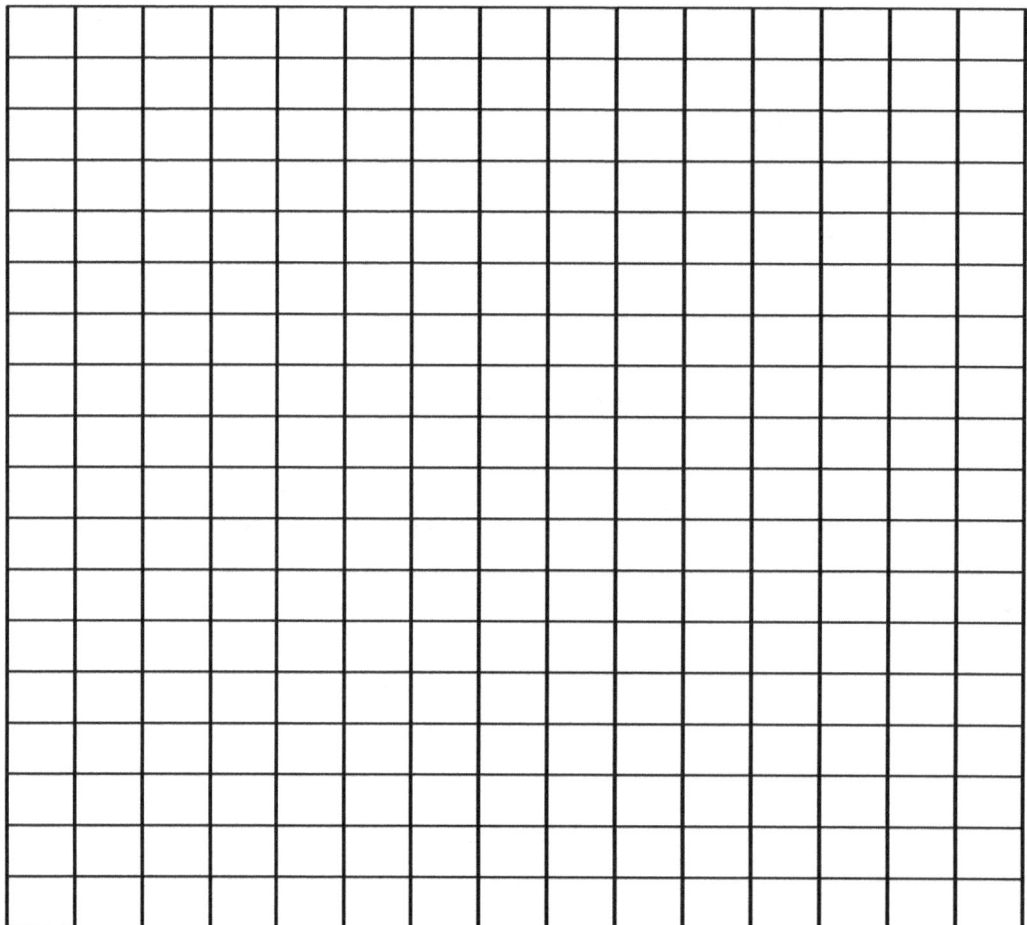

(Ch 4.1)

Y - axis (count by 20's)

Y - axis

Label your ordered pairs on the graph

X - axis _____

X - axis (Count by 5's)

(Chapter 5.1) Using the table on the previous page, <u>**derive the slope**</u>. <u>**Show all work below and place your answer in the box**</u>.

Slope (m) =

(Chapter 5.2/5.3) Using the slope above, formulate an equation in <u>**Slope-Intercept form.**</u> Show all work below and place your answer in the box.

Slope-Intercept form Answer using function notation (Ch 4.7):

Line of Best Fit (Linear Regression) Using Technology (S.ID.8)

L_1	L_2

<u>Calculator Window</u>

Xmin =   Xscl =   Ymax =   Xres =

Xmax =   Ymin =   Yscl =

<u>Line of Best Fit/Linear Regression</u>
(Write Linear Regression Equation below (for y)
subsituting values)

a =

b =

y =

r =

In the space to the below, elaborate on the **relationship** between the numerical value of the correlation coefficient and what it means in context to your data.

_____

_____

_____

Push the "Y=" button now plug the equation you derived from the slope-intercept form on the bottom of Pg. 229 into the calculator for (Y_2). Once that is completed push the "graph" button to compare **your** equation versus the **calculator's** linear regression. **Find me when finished to be checked off.**

My box to check off.

Directions - Generate an equation based on the data below.
Photogate at 40 cm and Speed at 241 cm/s. Photogate at 50 cm and Speed at 267 cm/s.
- Show mathematical work below.

Original Equation using function notation Ch 5.5:

(Domain - Start from 0 and Count by 15's)
(Range - Round to the ones place)

Use the equation above
to complete the table below.

Domain	Function	Range

Pg. 232

Graph the equation from Pg. 231 on the coordinate plane below.

Label your ordered pairs on the graph.

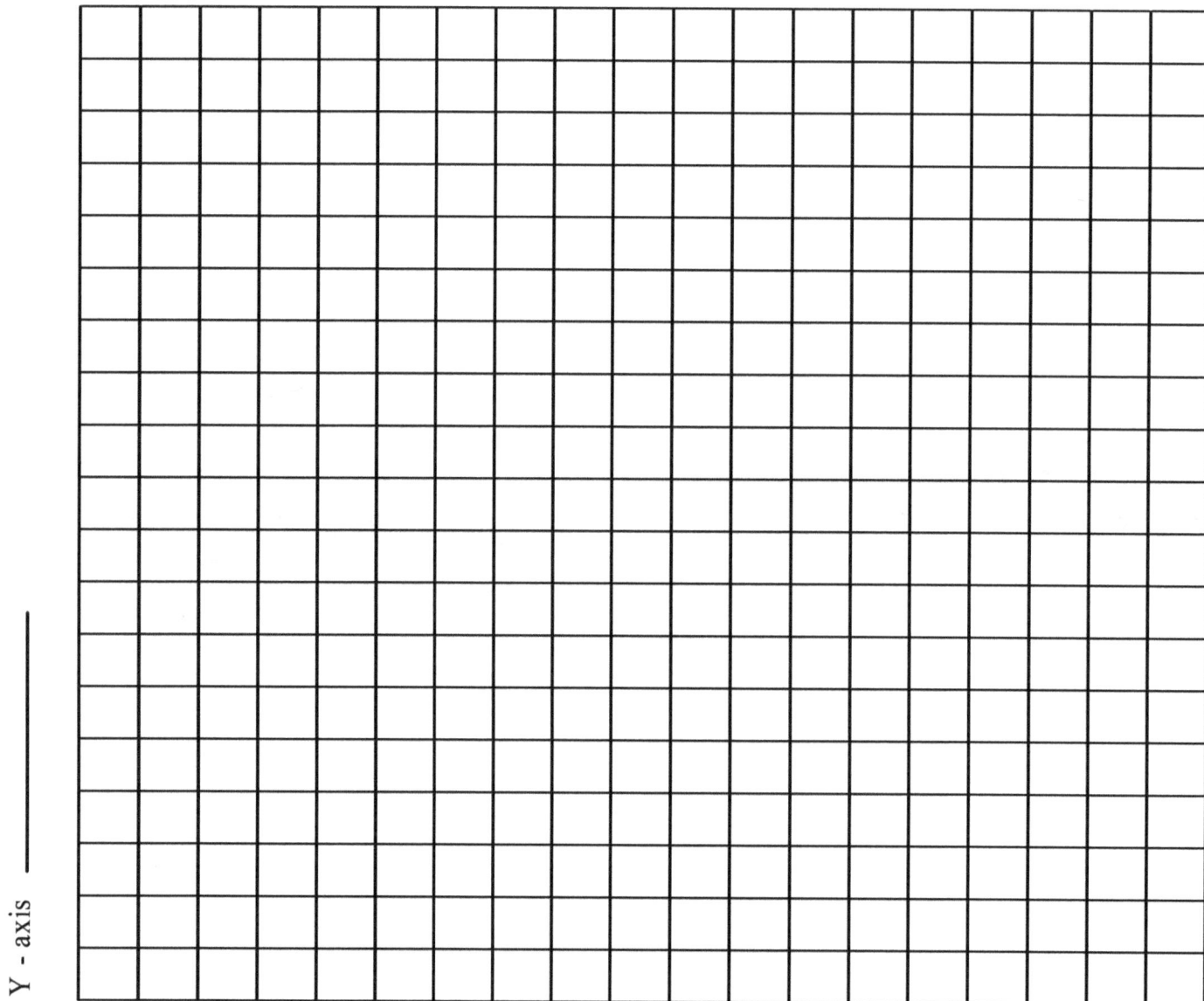

Y - axis

X - axis _____

**(Hint - X-axis count by 5's
Y-axis count by 10's)**

Directions - Generate an equation **Parallel** to the one given to you on Pg. 231 that goes through a point with Photogate at 30 cm and Speed at 180 cm/s. **(Ch 5.5)** - **Show mathematical work below.**

Parallel Line Equation using function notation Ch 5.5:

(Write in words below how you <u>know</u> your line is <u>parallel.</u>

(Domain - Start from 0 and Count by 15's)
(Range - Round to the ones place)

<u>*Use the parallel equation*</u>
<u>*above to complete the table below.*</u>

Domain	Function	Range

First, graph the equation from Pg. 231 **again** on the coordinate plane below. Then, **Graph** the **parallel line equation** on the same coordinate plane using the **3 column table on the previous page.**

Label your ordered pairs on the graph.   **Ch 5.5**

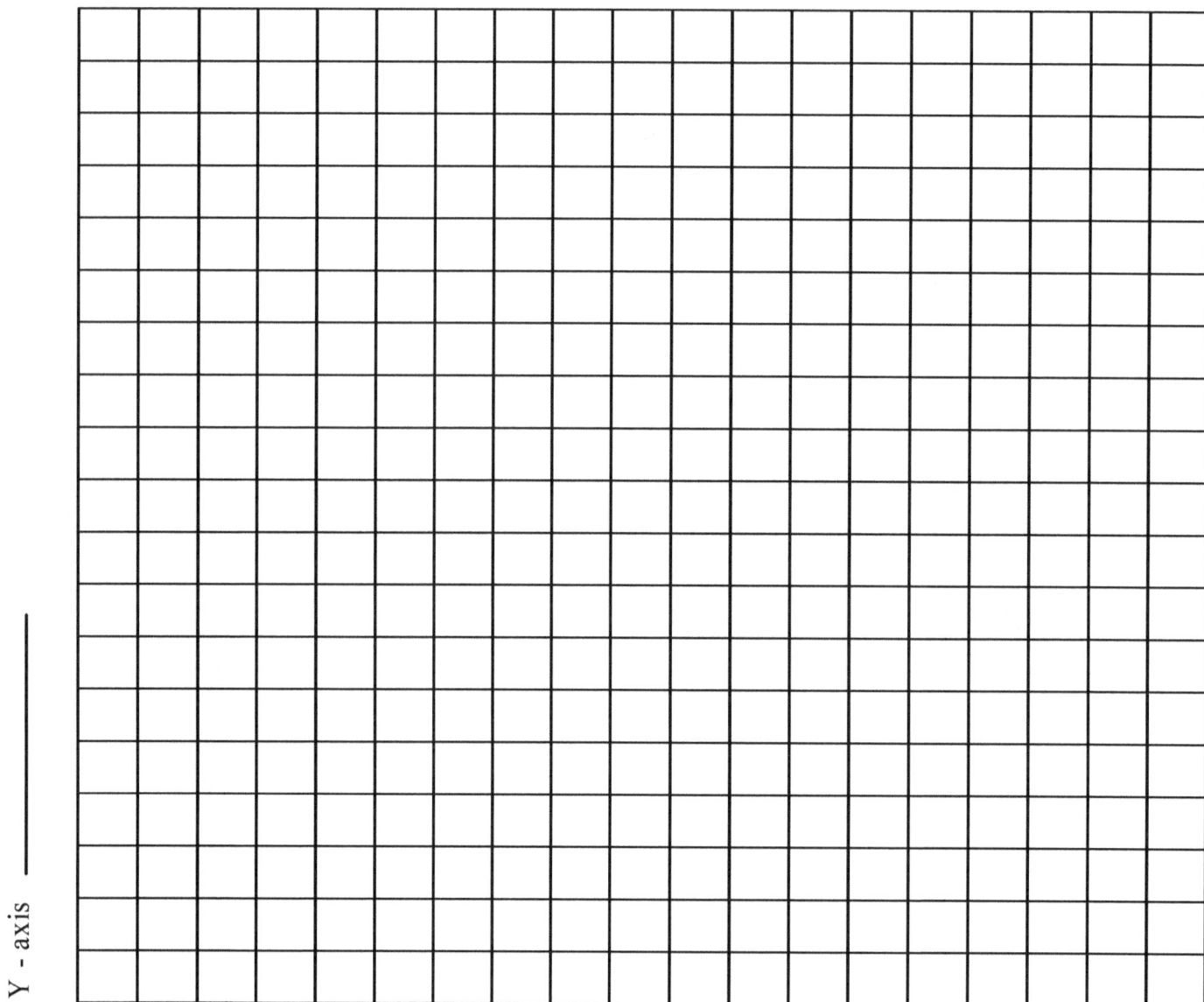

Y - axis

X - axis _____

(Hint - X-axis count by 5's
       Y-axis count by 10's)

Directions - Generate an equation **Perpendicular** to the one given to you on Pg. 231 that goes through a point with photogate at 70 cm and speed at 120 cm/s. **(Ch 5.5)**
- **Show mathematical work below.**

Perpendicular Line Equation using function notation Ch 5.5:

(**Write in words below how you know your line is perpendicular** - Also, what is the **product** of their slopes).

(Domain - Start from 0 and Count by 15's)
(Range - Round to the ones place)

Use the perpendicular equation above to complete the table below.

Domain	Function	Range

Pg. 236

First, graph the equation from Pg. 231 **again** on the coordinate plane below. Then,
Graph the **perpendicular line equation** on the same coordinate plane using the
3 column table on the previous page.

Label your ordered pairs on the graph (estimate the intersection point)

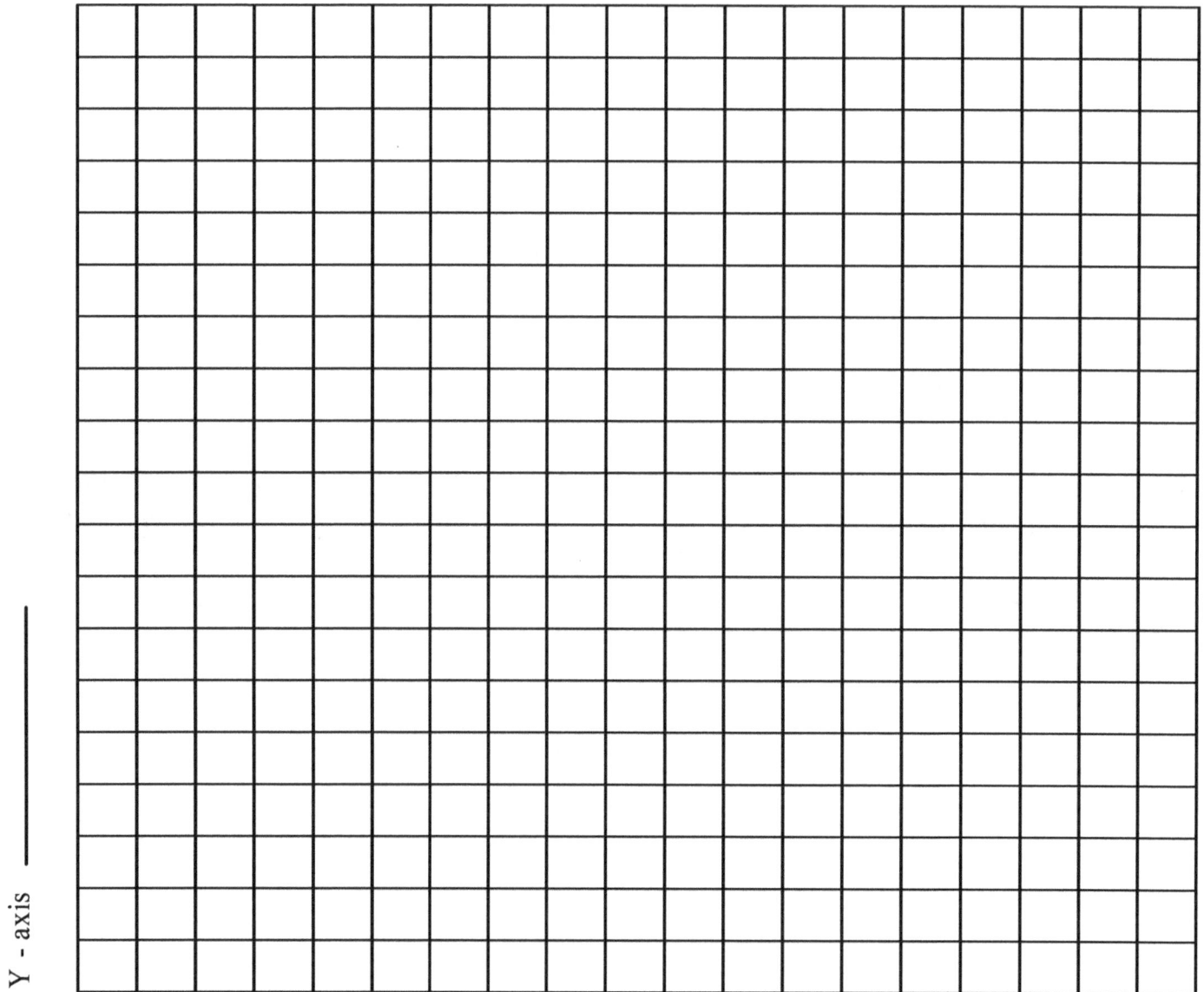

Y - axis

X - axis _____

**(Hint - X-axis count by 5's
Y-axis count by 20's)**

Estimated ordered pair of intersection point

(,   )

In the space provided at the bottom of the page, set up the two equations below as a System of Equations and find the solution. Round solutions to the nearest hundredth place.

Pg. 231 Original Equation:

Pg. 235 Perpendicular Equation:

Solution:

Elaborate on the context of your solution above._____

_____

_____

Type the two equations below into the "y =" button on your calculator.

Pg. 231 Original Equation (Y$_1$):

Pg. 235 Perpendicular Equation (Y$_2$):

Original Equation (Use coordinates from Pg. 231)	**Calculator Window**	**Perpendicular Equation** (Use coordinates from Pg. 235)

L$_1$	L$_2$

Xmin =

Xmax =

Xscl =

Ymax =

Ymin =

Yscl =

Xres =

L$_1$	L$_3$

Once you have plugged in all the data above into your calculator select "GRAPH". You should see both sets of points with lines going through them. If you do not see them, be creative and find a way, if that does not work then ask me. Once you see both, select "2nd", then "TRACE". This will send you to "CALC" which sets up different components to solve for. Select "5" - Intersection (which is the solution to both graphs). Move your cursor near the intersection using the arrow keys and hit enter 3 times.

Write the solution rounded to the hundredths place below.

Solution:

How close is your solution to the calculator's? Calculate the differences in x - values and y - values from pages 237 and 238 then write the findings below. **Find me when you are finished so that I can check this page off.**

Differences in x-values:

My box to check off.

Differences in y-values:

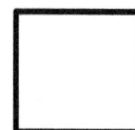

> **Pg. 233 Parallel Equation using function notation (Type into Y$_3$):**

s(85) =

Using the notation above, write a question that needs to be solved.

_____

s(85) =

Below, show the work needed to find the solution.

Ordered Pair

(   )

My box to check off.

The x - Value in context _____.

The s(x) - Value in context _____.

> **Pg. 235 Perpendicular Equation using function notation (Type into Y$_2$):**

s(x) = 300   x =

Using the notation above, write a question that needs to be solved.

_____

s(x) = 300   x =

Below, show the work needed to find the solution.

Ordered Pair

(   )

My box to check off.

The x - Value in context _____.

The s(x) - Value in context _____.

Pg. 240

Ch 4.3

We have paid $9,000 for the car and ramp sets that you are using. The car and ramps together were $500. Each photogate was $850. Let X be the car and ramp price and Y be the price of the photogates. Round # of photogates to the most sensible ones place.

# of car and ramps (X)	Value of car and ramps	Funds left for photogates	# of photogates (Y)
0			
			$\frac{0}{-} =$

From the first 4 rows of the table above, generate an equation to find the number of photogates purchased as a function of the number of car and ramps purchased.

_____

What does the x - intercept mean in context of the problem? (Write ordered pair)

_____

What does the y - intercept mean in context of the problem? (Write ordered pair)

_____

Y axis

(start at 2, count by odd #'s)

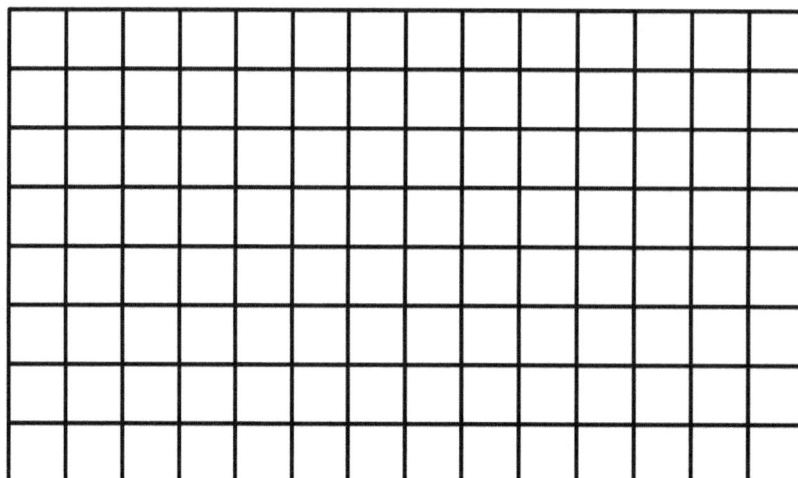

Label your x/y intercepts on the graph.

X axis (count by 2's)

Take your data from the Slope Intercept equation at the bottom of Pg. 229 and do the following:

- Write your **Slope-Intercept Form** Answer from Pg. 229 below.

- **Graph** your equation using the **Y-Intercept** and **Slope** below.

Ch 4.5

Label your ordered pairs on the graph

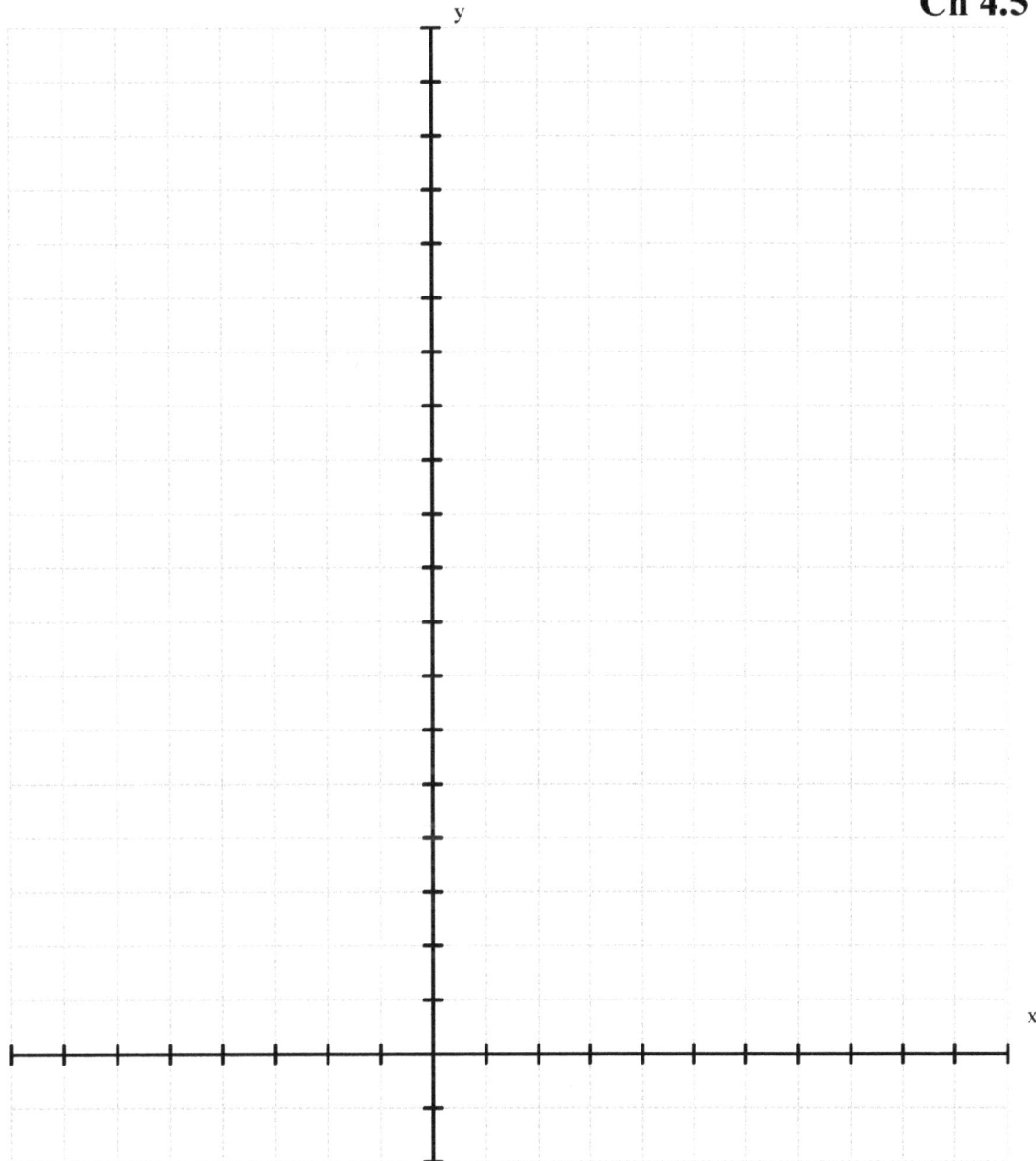

For your x and y axes, number them however you need to in order to **graph** at least 6 points. **Make sure you connect all possible points.**
List 6 consecutive ordered pairs below.

Blank page for additional space to show work, to write additional thoughts that come to mind, or to doodle if necessary.

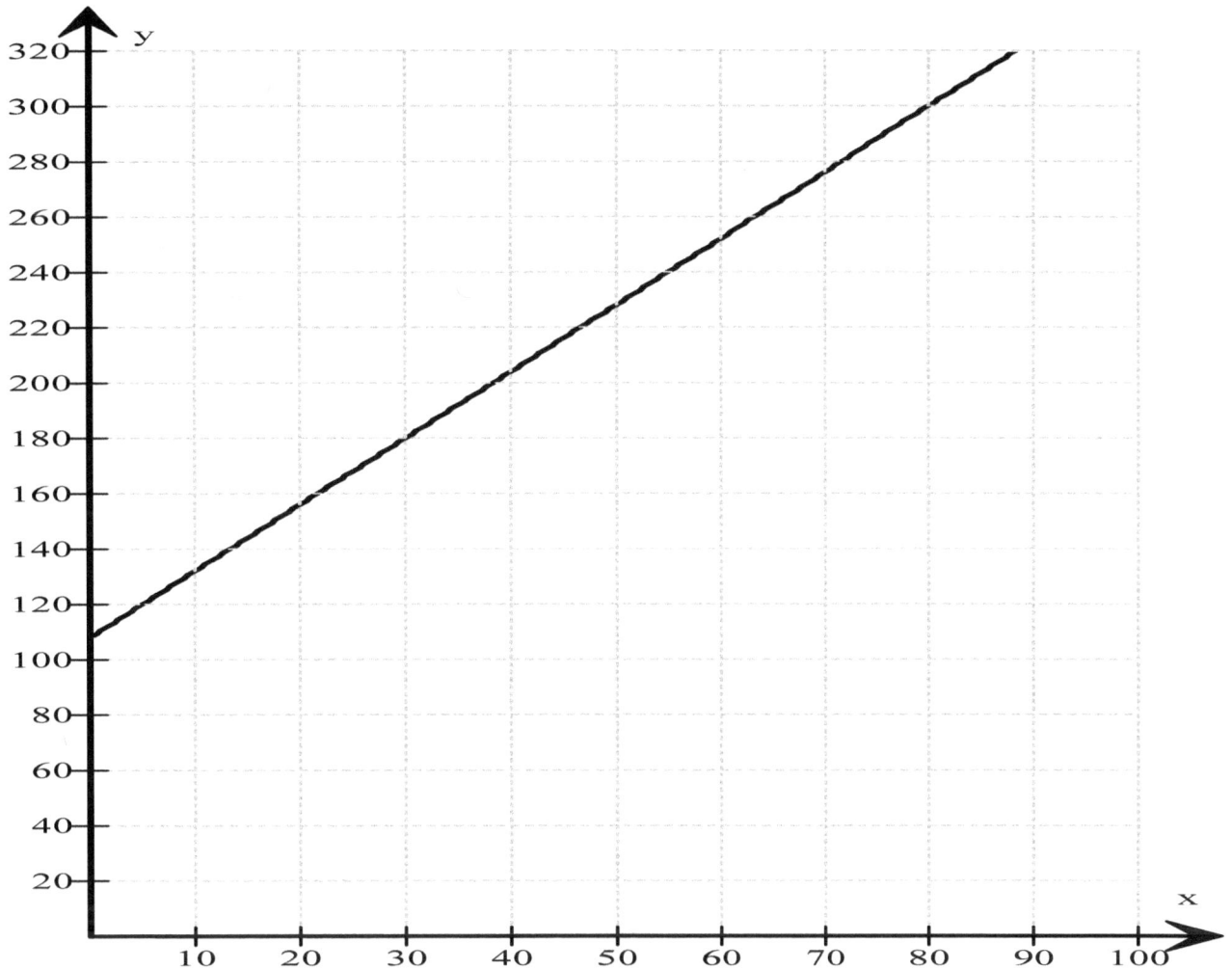

Use the graph above to answer questions 1 and 2. Use the words input and output when describing your solution in context.

1) s(60) = _____   Ordered Pair (   )

Write your total solution in context:_____

_____

2) s(x) ≈ 136 cm/s; x = _____   Ordered Pair (   )

Write your total solution in context:_____

_____

Grading Scales for all Chapters Covered in this Benchmark

- This is how I grade your benchmark. Do not worry about these pages until after I grade it.
- Refer to all scales previously passed out for each chapter to understand exactly what each score represents.
- Remember, there is No reason to guess in this classroom.

Chapter 1.6: Functions and Tables - Pg. 228

4	3.5	3	2.5	2	1.5	1

Chapter 4.1: Graphing on a Coordinate Plane - Pg. 228

4	3.5	3	2.5	2	1.5	1

Chapter 5.1: Slope Formula - Pg. 229

4	3.5	3	2.5	2	1.5	1

Chapter 5.2/5.3: Slope Intercept Form - Pg. 229

4	3.5	3	2.5	2	1.5	1

S.ID. 8: Linear Regression Using Technology - Pg. 230

4	3.5	3	2.5	2	1.5	1

Chapter 4.2: Graphing Linear Equations from Data - Pg. 231 & 232

4	3.5	3	2.5	2	1.5	1

Chapter 5.5: Write and Graph Equations of Parallel Lines - Pg. 233 & 234

4	3.5	3	2.5	2	1.5	1

Chapter 5.5: Write/Graph Equations of Perpendicular Lines - Pg. 235 & 236

4	3.5	3	2.5	2	1.5	1

Chapter 7.2: Solving Linear Systems - Pg. 237 & 238

4	3.5	3	2.5	2	1.5	1

Chapter 4.7: Function Notation (Application) - Pg. 239 & 243

4	3.5	3	2.5	2	1.5	1

Chapter 4.3: X and Y Intercepts in Context - Pg. 240

4	3.5	3	2.5	2	1.5	1

Chapter 4.5: Graphing in Slope and Y-intercept Form - Pg. 241

4	3.5	3	2.5	2	1.5	1

Pg. 246

Blank Page for notes, thoughts,

Or drawings.

Name_____ Period_____ Date_____

Analysis of Car and Ramp Guiding Questions

1) What are ways we can create linear equations that describe relationships? (Provide Examples)

_____

_____

_____

_____

_____

_____

_____

_____

This empty space is for illustrations you may want to add.

2). What is the **relationship** between the numerical value of the correlation coefficient and what it means in context of your data? (Provide Examples)

_____

_____

_____

_____

_____

_____

_____

_____

_____

This empty space is for illustrations you may want to add.

3) How does the concept of a function and function notation apply to individual units?

_____

_____

_____

_____

_____

_____

_____

_____

_____

This empty space is for illustrations you may want to add.

4) What are the processes needed to **graphically** represent linear equations?

_____

_____

_____

_____

_____

_____

_____

_____

_____

This empty space is for illustrations you may want to add.

Guiding Questions	1) Struggling	2) Basic	3) Proficient	4) Mastery
What are ways we can create linear equations that describe relationships?	**Student's explanation** of how linear equations can be created that describe relationships **was very minimal or non-existent. Student's use of vocabulary terms is confusing or non-existent and either provides an illustration that does not support their answer or does not provide an illustration at all.**	Student **has a basic explanation on just one way or more than one way** linear equations can be created that describe relationships. **Student uses vocabulary terms somewhat correctly and provides a very limited illustration to support their answer.**	Student **has a detailed explanation on just one way** linear equations can be created that describe relationships. **Student uses a few vocabulary terms correctly and provides a good illustration to support their answer.**	Student **lists and has detailed explanations for more than one way** linear equations can be created that describe relationships. **Student uses a variety of vocabulary terms precisely and provides a thorough illustration to support their answer.**
What are the relationships between the numerical value of the correlation coefficient and what it means in context?	Student **is not able to make the connection** between the numerical value of the correlation coefficient and what it means in context. **Student's use of vocabulary terms is confusing or non-existent and either provides an illustration that does not support their answer or does not provide an illustration at all.**	Student **has difficulty making the connection** between the numerical value of the correlation coefficient and what it means in context. **Student uses vocabulary terms somewhat correctly and provides a very limited illustration to support their answer.**	Student provides an **adequate connection** between the numerical value of the correlation coefficient and what it means in context. **Student uses a few vocabulary terms correctly and provides a good illustration to support their answer.**	Student provides a **precise connection** between the numerical value of the correlation coefficient and what it means in context. **Student uses a variety of vocabulary terms precisely and provides a thorough illustration to support their answer.**
How does the concept of a function and function notation apply to individual units?	Student **is not able to relate** how the concept of a function and function notation applies to individual units. **Student's use of vocabulary terms is confusing or non-existent and either provides an illustration that does not support their answer or does not provide an illustration at all.**	Student **has difficulty relating** how the concept of a function and function notation applies to individual units. **Student uses vocabulary terms somewhat correctly and provides a very limited illustration to support their answer.**	Student provides an **adequate answer relating** how the concept of a function and function notation applies to individual units. **Student uses a few vocabulary terms correctly and provides a good illustration to support their answer.**	Student provides a **precise answer relating** how the concept of a function and function notation applies to individual units **Student uses a variety of vocabulary terms precisely and provides a thorough illustration to support their answer.**
What are the processes needed to graphically represent linear equations?	Student's explanation on processes needed to graphically represent linear equations **was very minimal or non-existent. Student's use of vocabulary terms is confusing or non-existent and either provides an illustration that does not support their answer or does not provide an illustration at all.**	Student **has a basic explanation on just one process or more than one** process needed to graphically represent linear equations. **Student uses vocabulary terms somewhat correctly and provides a very limited illustration to support their answer.**	Student **has a detailed explanation on just one** processes needed to graphically represent linear equations. **Student uses a few vocabulary terms correctly and provides a good illustration to support their answer.**	Student **lists and has detailed explanations for explaining more than one** process needed to graphically represent linear equations. **Student uses a variety of vocabulary terms precisely and provides a thorough illustration to support their answer.**

Pg. 252

Blank Page for notes, thoughts,

Or drawings.

Full Name_____ Period_____ Date_____

Car and Ramp "Linear Equation/Graphing" Vocabulary Exam

I _____, hereby state the answers I am providing are my own. I have not looked at any other classmate's quiz/test and/or re-copy answers from an unauthorized sheet of paper. By me signing this, if I get caught cheating, I am acknowledging the fact I will receive a "Fail" for this exam and will not be able to re-take it. If I do not sign my exam will not be graded.

1) What are the 4 different types of slopes and the visual characteristics of each type of graph.
(+4 points: names of slopes; +4 points: correct graphs)

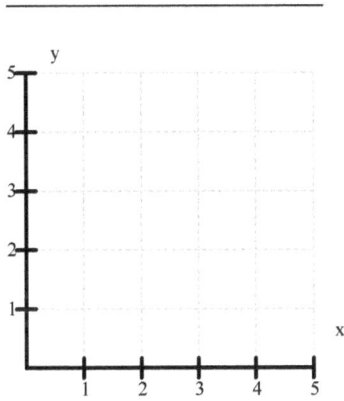

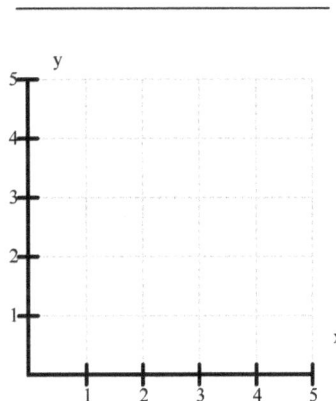

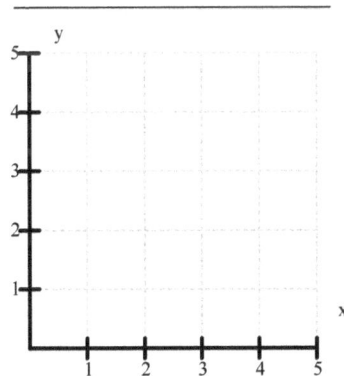

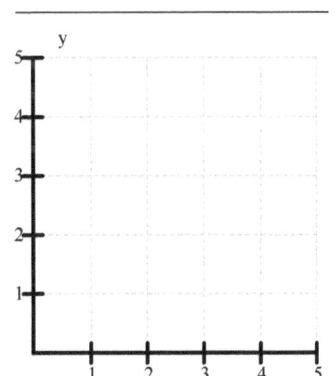

_____   _____

_____   _____

2) Write the point slope formula
(+1 point)

_____

3) Write the formula to find the slope if given two points.
(+1 point)

_____

4)

• What is the name of the following formula: $y = mx + b$

_____

(+1 point)

• The "b" in $y = mx + b$ is the symbol for the_____ **(+1 point)**

• The "b" is what point on the graph of an equation?_____

_____

(+1 point)

5) Correlation Coefficient

• If your "r" is .32 state the following:

_____ Relationship **(+1 point)**

• Describe the relationship between X and Y.

_____

_____

(+1 point)

• Draw a graph representing the relationship between X and Y **(+1 point)**

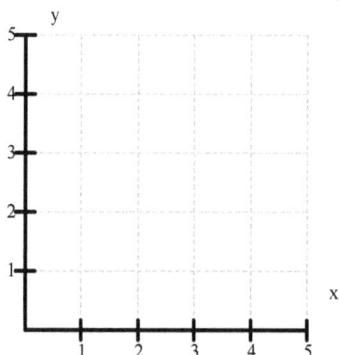

6) Correlation Coefficient

- If your "r" is -.63 state the following:

_____ Relationship **(+1 point)**

- Describe the relationship between X and Y.

_____

_____
(+1 point)

- Draw a graph representing the relationship between X and Y **(+1 point)**

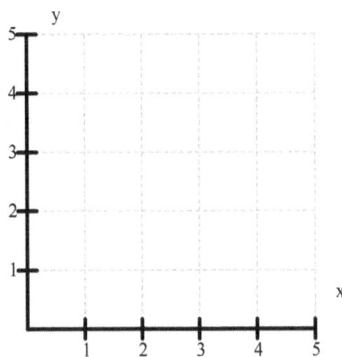

7) If a graph is a function which variable cannot repeat _____.
(+1 point)

8) The set of all x-values are called the _____. **(+1 pt)**

The set of all y-values are called the_____. **(+1 pt)**

Parallel and Perpendicular Equations
9) _____ equations have the same_____ but different
_____.**(+3 points)**

10) _____ equations have slopes that are _____

_____
of each other. **(+3 points)**

11) The product of two perpendicular slopes is _____. **(+1 point)**

12) What method will we use when solving a system of equations?

_____ **(+1 point)**

13) What is the solution of a systems of equations called?

_____ **(+1 point)**

14) When "y" is replaced with *f(x)* to describe a function, *f(x)* is called

_____ **(+1 point)**

Grading
(there are 32 points total)

+32 = 4.0

+28 to +31 = 3.5

+25 to +27 = 3.0

+19 to +24 = 2.0

+16 to +18 = 1.0

+0 to + 15 = 0

Points Correct_____

Scale Percentage_____

TI 83 Line of Best Fit

Produces a scatterplot, and then a line of best fit for a table of data involving two variables.

1. Press STAT (left of arrow buttons)
2. Press 1:Edit (or press ENTER since 1 is the default choice)

```
EDIT CALC TESTS
1:Edit…
2:SortA(
3:SortD(
4:ClrList
5:SetUpEditor
```

3. If the list has data in it already, as shown below, you can clear the list(s)

```
L1      L2      L3     2
3546    19      ------
2795    23
2600    23
3515    19
3245    23
3930    17
3115    20

L2(1)=19
```

To clear a list,

a. Press STAT button

```
EDIT CALC TESTS
1:Edit…
2:SortA(
3:SortD(
4:ClrList
5:SetUpEditor
```

b. Press 4 to choose 4:ClrList

```
ClrList
```

c. Press 2nd and the 1 key (which will enter a L_1 if you want to erase List 1)

d. Press ENTER and you will see this

```
ClrList L1
            Done
```

e. Repeat steps a through d until all the lists you want cleared are clear. To clear list 2, in step c you would press 2nd and the 2 key, and so on. You can also clear several at one time by entering commas between list names as in

```
ClrList L1
            Done
ClrList L2
            Done
ClrList L1,L2
            Done
```

4. If you had to clear lists, you need to repeat steps 1 and 2 to see empty lists ready to be filled. (Steps 1 and 2: Press $\boxed{\text{STAT}}$ and $\boxed{\text{ENTER}}$)

L1	L2	L3	1
	------	------	

L1(1)=

5. Start entering data into L1, pressing $\boxed{\text{ENTER}}$ after each item. L1 is using the x value from each (x,y) pair. Examples are shown below.

6. When you are done with L1, use the right arrow key, $\boxed{\bullet}$, to get into L2

L1	L2	L3	2
1		------	
2			
3			
4			
5			
6			
7			

L2(1)=

7. Enter the L2 data, pressing $\boxed{\text{ENTER}}$ after each item. Some sample data is below.

L1	L2	L3	3
1	5		
2	11		
3	14		
4	18		
5	28		
6	30		
7	37		

L3(1)=

8. You may need to adjust the Window to fit your data. Press the $\boxed{\text{WINDOW}}$ key (beside the Y= key)

    a. In our case, the Ymax is not big enough. You can change those values.

9. Before you graph, you should turn off any graphs in the $\boxed{\text{Y=}}$ window.

a. Press the [Y=] key.

```
Plot1  Plot2  Plot3
\Y1■sin(X)
\Y2■X/315
\Y3=
\Y4=
\Y5=
\Y6=
\Y7=
```

b. Drag the cursor over the highlighted = and press [ENTER]. This will 'turn off' the graphs of those functions without you having to erase that function. You will lose the Y1 function during the best fit process.

```
Plot1  Plot2  Plot3
\Y1=sin(X)
\Y2=X/315
\Y3=
\Y4=
\Y5=
\Y6=
\Y7=
```

10. You need to turn on the scatter plot function.
   a. Press [2nd] and the [Y=] key (to turn on the STAT PLOT)
   b. Press [ENTER] to choose Plot 1
   c. Press [ENTER] again while the cursor is over the On.
   d. Make sure that your Xlist is L1 and your Ylist is L2

```
Plot1  Plot2  Plot3
On  Off
Type: ▦ ⬈ ⬛
      ⬛ ⬛ ⬈
Xlist:L1
Ylist:L2
Mark: ■ + ·
```

11. Press the [GRAPH] key

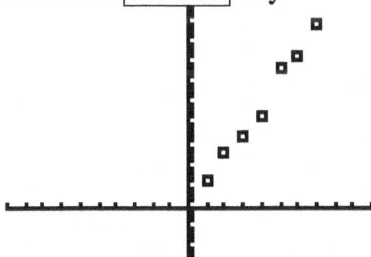

12. Now we will try to find the line of Best Fit. We're going to try to fit it to a straight line. Other types of functions could be used (fit it to a quadratic eqation, or a cubic, or a natural log,....)
   a. Press the [STAT] key

b. Arrow over to the $\boxed{\text{CALC}}$ menu

c. Press $\boxed{4}$ to choose 4:LinReg(ax + b) **(We will choose 8: LinReg(a + bx)**

d. Press $\boxed{2^{nd}}$ and the $\boxed{1}$ key to get L1
e. Press the comma key $\boxed{,}$
f. Press $\boxed{2^{nd}}$ and the $\boxed{2}$ key to get L2
g. Press the comma key $\boxed{,}$
h. Press the $\boxed{\text{VARS}}$ key (below the arrows, next to $\boxed{\text{CLEAR}}$)
i. Arrow over to Y-VARS

(If you have a TI-84, steps d-g you will not do. Once you press #8 you will input your "x-values" list into the "Xlist" and the "y-values" list into the "Ylist")
(You will then scroll down to "Store RegEQ" then complete steps h to k)

j. Press $\boxed{\text{ENTER}}$ to choose 1:Function and see

```
FUNCTION
1:Y₁
2:Y₂
3:Y₃
4:Y₄
5:Y₅
6:Y₆
7↓Y₇
```

k. Press $\boxed{\text{ENTER}}$ again to select Y1

l. Press $\boxed{\text{ENTER}}$ again to process your request and you will see our line of best fit is approximately y = 5.29x – 0.71

The close |r| is to 1, the better fit you have.

13. Press the GRAPH key to see your best fit line together with your scatter plot.

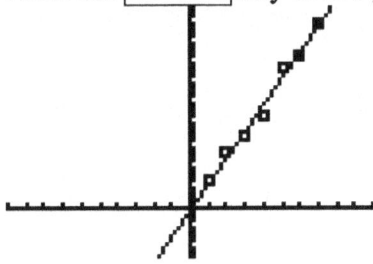

14. You can also see your line of best fit as Y1 if you press the Y= button.

www.ingramcontent.com/pod-product-compliance
Lightning Source LLC
LaVergne TN
LVHW061335060426
835511LV00014B/1936